writing ,
your story's
THEME

The Writers' Guide
to Plotting Stories That Matter

writing your story's
THEME

The Writer's Guide to Plotting Stories That Matter

K.M. WEILAND

Writing Your Story's Theme

Published by PenForASword Publishing.

ISBN-13: 978-1-944936-11-2

TABLE OF CONTENTS

Introduction

THEME = CHARACTER = PLOT

ONCE UPON A time, Character fell in love with Plot. Right from the start it was a stormy relationship. There was passion, there was romance, there were epic stakes. Sometimes they were pretty sure they couldn't live with each other a moment longer. Sometimes they tried to give each other up altogether. But even the most resolute intentions couldn't keep them apart for longer than a lukewarm novel or two. Inevitably, these star-crossed lovers always reunited, their reincarnations seeking each other out again and again through the ages.

They never seemed to realize Theme watched them from afar, love largely unrequited. During all the glory days when fans fervently debated Plot versus Character, Theme was the one who secretly made the relationship work. Toiling silently behind the scenes, Theme kept pushing Plot and Character together, even when they thought they hated each other. Theme gave meaning to their union. Theme made them a team.

And so goes the greatest love triangle in all fiction.

***

Like some new chicken-and-egg debate, writers frequently weigh the respective merits of plot and character. Which came first? Which is more important? Which is the hallmark of the truly great stories?

This debate, however, is a false paradigm.

For starters, it's a dilemma with no conclusive answer, since character-driven fiction offers one array of fictional techniques and plot-driven fiction another, both equally valid. Even more importantly, this type of either/or questioning tends to ignore the fact that character and plot's relationship is part of a larger triangle—crowned by none other than wispy, metaphysical, powerful, unavoidable theme.

Why is theme so often excluded from the grand tug of war between plot and character?

There are a couple reasons.

The most obvious is simply that writers often don't view theme in the same category as plot and character. Plot and character are concrete pieces of story, while theme seems more abstract. Plot and character are almost always discussed in terms of technique: "This is how you do it, kids..." Theme, on the other hand, is often referenced with vague hand gestures: "Oh, you know, it just sort of happens..."

Some authors turn this principle of Thematic Vagueness into a kind of religion. When eager new writers look on high for answers about theme ("How do I write a story with a strong theme?"), the responses are adamantly mysterious ("Thou shalt never write theme on purpose").

The mysteriousness arises from a poor comprehension of how theme functions and interacts with other major story components. Because poorly executed themes are often those that are most obvious and on the nose, writers sometimes scare themselves off the subject altogether. We evolve from a healthy fear of preachy themes to an irrational avoidance of theme altogether.

It's true that powerful, cohesive themes sometimes emerge naturally from a writer's unconscious. But what's even truer is that these seemingly instinctive themes emerge thanks to the author's *intentional understanding and use* of those other storytelling titans: plot and character.

There lies the secret. If you can execute your plot and character arcs with understanding and intention, you're *this close* to extending that consciousness to theme itself. No more hoping and praying your unconscious talks to you in a way you understand well enough to transcribe. No more confusion about why your excellent plot and awesome characters sometimes refuse to play nice and combine into an equally amazing story. No more worrying that readers will find your story soulless or (just as bad) a self-righteous sermon.

Instead, you can bring theme out of the mists and let it work in the daylight, allowing it to guide your every story decision.

In my opening allegory, I cast plot, character, and theme as a triangle. But perhaps a more helpful figure is that of a circle—representing the unending, regenerative relationship of fiction's Big Three.

Plot, character, and theme are not individual, isolated aspects of story. As such, they cannot be developed in isolation. Rather, they are parts in a larger symbiosis.

Theme isn't just a nice greeting-card sentiment randomly mouthed by the protagonist at some point. Rather, theme creates character, which in turn creates plot, which brings the circle all the way around and, in turn, generates theme, which creates character which creates plot which creates... ad infinitum.

Honestly, I geek out just thinking about it. Theme is meant to represent unifying patterns found within a larger whole, which means that even on a meta level, it makes total sense that theme is both generative and receptive in its relationship to plot and character.

In his classic *The Art of Fiction*, instructor John Gardner wrote:

> Theme ... is not imposed on the story but evoked from within it—initially an intuitive but finally an intellectual act on the part of the writer.

What this means is that you, the writer, have the ability to start with any one of the Big Three and use it to create cohesive manifestations in the other two. If you begin with a plot idea, then character and theme will already be inherent seeds within that kernel. If you begin with character? Same deal. And if you begin with theme? Ah, no more worries about preachiness. You now have the ability to craft powerful messages that are *shown* via your plot and character, rather than *told* to readers.

At some point, once you become accustomed to looking at plot, character, and theme as three faces of a greater whole, it becomes difficult to extricate one from the other enough to even identify which occurred to you first.

As a storyteller, your end goal should be a uniform big picture for readers. One of the most useful processes for reaching that goal is, in fact, mentally breaking down the larger picture and keeping its specific parts separate within your own mind. This alone will dispel the haze of ambiguity surrounding theme. Once you can see what each major piece of the story is and is not, you will have a better understanding of how they relate to and impact one another.

Naturally, this is a deep and nuanced subject—one that encompasses, among other things, all of plot structure and character arc. For starters, consider the following three (and a half) mirroring layers that can be found in almost every part of every story.

1a. Exterior Plot Action

This is usually represented in active/reactive behaviors from the protagonist (and other characters). This is what is *happening* in a story. It's the action your characters experience and your readers visualize.

For Example:

Inman is journeying home in *Cold Mountain*.

Juliet is talking to the islanders about their experiences during World War II in *The Guernsey Literary and Potato Peel Pie Society*.

WRITING YOUR STORY'S THEME | 13

Sydney Carton is rescuing Charles Darnay in *A Tale of Two Cities*.

Kaladin is fighting as a slave in the never-ending war on the Shattered Plains in *The Way of Kings*.

1b. Main Conflict

Usually, the main conflict is part and parcel of the exterior plot action; however, because it often manifests differently, it's worth considering as a layer of its own. Whereas the exterior plot action is usually physical in some sense, the main conflict is often represented on a mental level. Effectively, it is a puzzle for the protagonist to solve. It may be an outright mystery or it may simply be a series of goals/conflicts/outcomes that progressively teach the protagonist how to reach the ultimate plot goal.

For Example:

Inman figures out how to get home, both by learning to navigate the mountains and by deducing how to get past the obstacles presented by each person he meets on his way.

Juliet figures out on a general level how to convince the islanders to talk to her, while in pursuit of the more specific mystery of what happened to the missing Elizabeth McKenna.

Sydney comes up with a plan to journey to France and rescue Charles.

Kaladin figures out how to survive as first a slave, then a soldier.

2. Character Arc

The character arc (usually although not necessarily exclusively the protagonist's) represents the inner conflict, which will, in turn, catalyze and/or be catalyzed by the outer conflict as presented in the plot's external action.

Note that we started our list with the top layer—the most obvious layer—of plot. But as we dig deeper into successive layers, we get closer to the heart of the story. If you think of a story's plot action as an externalized metaphor for the character's inner conflict and growth, you will have discovered one of the key ways in which the abstraction of theme is made concrete within the actual story.

For Example:

Inman battles his own doubt and suffering in his overwhelming desire to escape the American Civil War and get home to his sweetheart Ada.

Juliet begins falling in love with Guernsey in general and the kind but taciturn Dawsey in particular.

Sydney struggles with saving Darnay for Lucie, since it means cutting off any hope of his being with the woman he loves.

Kaladin's bitterness over his lot and his hatred for those who enslaved him vie with his inherent nobility and his natural leadership skills.

3. Theme

Now we hit bedrock. As the least visible but most important of a story's layers, theme is the realization of all that has gone before. It is the symbolic argument between a posited Truth and Lie, which will be played out in the protagonist's personal arc and throughout the external plot (which, in its turn, has forced the character's growth).

For Example:

Out of Inman's and Ada's separate struggles and ultimately futile attempts to be together arises an introspective theme about the search for meaning in the face of suffering.

By falling in love with the simple valor and loyalty found in Guernsey's people, Juliet finally discovers purpose and meaning in her own life.

In ultimately sacrificing himself in Darnay's stead, Sydney surrenders his dissipated life in exchange for "a far, far better rest ... than I have ever known."

Kaladin's struggle to overcome his bitterness and hatred —mirrored, contrasted, and finally aided by the many characters around him—culminates in a growing commitment to selfless leadership.

As you can see, although these elements are most visible in the stated order (plot, character, theme), their importance in defining the story is actually the reverse.

No matter what type of story you write, its success will arise from the balance of its three most important pieces: plot, character, and theme. When you work on any one of these, you are necessarily working on all three. If you can raise them all into purposeful synchronicity as you write, you will not only bring theme out of the shadows, you will also be able to craft stories of deep meaning and purpose.

"To produce a mighty book,
you must choose a mighty theme.
No great and enduring volume
can ever be written on the flea,
though many there be that have tried it."
—Herman Melville

1

DISCOVERING YOUR
THEMATIC PRINCIPLE

THERE ARE WORDS I think of as "infinite words." These are words that express more in their essence than we can ever quite seem to explain. They're the words of poetry. Indeed, many are complete poems all in a single word.

To me, "theme" is such a word.

It is one of those endlessly fascinating subjects you can study all your life and never quite nail down. You circle it many times and think you've captured it in some neat little formula, only to discover you've seen just one of its faces, one of its many ambiguous and numinous aspects.

That's fun.

It's also frustrating.

For a writer—or indeed any artist—our finite relationship to the infinitude of theme can often feel akin to facing down the night sky in an attempt to understand the universe. As with so much of writing, we either go mad or realize "the struggle is the glory."

One of the reasons theme is so tricky to master is that it is also tricky to talk about. Because it is such a vast and abstract subject, every writer seems to have a slightly different definition. I learned this first-hand via the many Writing Questions of the Day (#WQOTD) I've conducted on Twitter and Facebook over the years. One of the questions I occasionally ask is simply, "What's your story's theme?"

The responses span the gamut from writers who rattle off single-word summations (such as "Responsibility") to writers who fret because they *can't* confine their themes to a single word. My personal preference for summing up theme is to look for the "Truth" at the heart of any prominent character change within the plot. But other authors will, with equal validity, choose instead to identify underlying topics or recurring motifs, many of which are never made explicit within the narrative.

This panoply of subtly different approaches can create confusion about what theme actually is. Every single one of these approaches seems legit. And they *are* legit—because every single one, although not necessarily definitive in itself, helps us gain a bigger-picture view of *story*. Just as importantly, each view provides metrics by which we can consciously analyze and perfect what we're doing.

In future chapters, we're going to look at theme through the lenses of plot and character, which will help us see its more specific and explicit manifestations. But first we need to enter the subject through the doorway of theme itself.

"Theme itself" is perhaps best summed up by its simplest definition:

> Theme is a unifying idea or subject, explored via recurring patterns and expanded through comparisons and contrasts.

Because theme in fiction often gets boxed into the narrow view of being nothing more than "the moral of the story," it's helpful to observe theme at work in different mediums. Consider music for example. Music is sheer emotion, manifesting in what is sometimes not just a mental or imaginative experience, but also a physical experience. Music tells stories and conveys truths without needing words.

French composer Pierre Schaeffer said:

> The moment at which music reveals its true nature is contained in the ancient exercise of the theme with

variations. The complete mystery of music is explained right there.

The same could be said for story. Although we parade it through various costumes of intellect, action, and sentiment, story is ultimately an expression of theme. The plot and the characters are just window dressing, providing visual metaphors for the author's underlying (and sometimes unconscious) ideas. If those ideas ring with universal truth, it will ultimately be the theme, more than the plot or the characters, that connects with readers.

YOUR STORY'S THEMATIC PRINCIPLE: WHAT IS IT?

The simplest way of expressing theme is via the thematic principle. The thematic principle may be a word, or it may be a sentence. Either way, your thematic principle is your story's "unifying idea." It is your story's representation and exploration of a universal Truth.

This Truth can take many forms:

- It may try to prove a **commonly held belief** ("wars are evil"), or try to **disprove an accepted belief** ("wars are a necessary evil").

- It may tackle the **deepest questions of human existence** ("why are we here?"), or explore our most **deeply held values** ("love is the most important thing").

- It may **offer answers**, either implicitly or explicitly ("love conquers all"), or it may choose only to **raise questions** ("does love conquer all?").

- It may focus on **moral dilemmas** ("is it okay to protect your own life at the expense of someone else's?"), or it may simply highlight **certain patterns** ("life in the inner city").

- It may choose to **comment** ("Nazi Germany was

immoral"), or it may attempt only to **observe** ("events of the Holocaust").

- It may choose a Truth that is **high-minded** ("life has meaning"), or it may be **mundane** ("high school is hard").

- It may be **optimistic** ("life is wonderful"), or it may be **pessimistic** ("humans are selfish").

The one thing the thematic principle *can't* be is vague. At first glance, this may seem an easily disprovable suggestion, since you can probably name great stories that seem thematically foggy. This is because excellent themes are rarely blatant or "on the nose." If a story works, you can be reasonably sure that however subtle its themes, they are neither vague nor accidental.

There is a huge difference between a *vague* theme, told by an author who was never quite sure what the theme was, versus a *subtle* theme that permeates every part of a story so completely it becomes almost invisible via its very prominence.

When I first investigated one of my favorite movies, John Sturges's classic film *The Great Escape*, I initially found it difficult to sum up a unifying thematic principle in any explicit statement. My go-to metric for finding a story's theme starts with identifying the Truth at the heart of the protagonist's arc, then looking for mirroring statements in every aspect of the story. But in some stories, like *The Great Escape*, the themes aren't so easily discovered (more on that in a minute).

Although condensing a story into a pithy "thematic principle" can sometimes seem overly simplistic, this is exactly what makes it a valuable tool. Your story's essence, boiled down to its most concise statement, can become the guiding principle for your entire project.

Once you have discovered what your story is about on a thematic level, you will be able to gut check every single scene, every character encounter, every bit of incidental symbolism. The more cohesive every single piece of your story becomes, the more powerful your theme becomes—and the more you can rely on overwhelming subtlety, via your plot and character arcs, rather than falling into heavy-handed moralizing.

As discussed previously, theme is rarely born in solitude. Theme ideas grow apace with plot ideas and character ideas. This means you do not have to identify your thematic principle in isolation. Identifying the *point* of your plot and the change in your characters will provide big flashing arrows aimed straight at your thematic principle.

For the moment, however, I want to talk about the thematic principle in isolation. Specifically, I want to examine some ways you can identify theme in stories where the plot and character arcs don't immediately seem to point to a unifying idea or Truth.

How to Identify a Story's Thematic Principle

Let's look back at *The Great Escape.* This is a true story, chronicling the tremendous effort of Allied airmen to escape a German prison camp during World War II. Despite its huge cast, it is less a character story than an event story. So what's the thematic principle? What Truth is this story sharing beyond that of a remarkable historical gambit?

On its surface, *The Great Escape* may seem to reflect the reason writers often feel theme should not be approached consciously. This is because when theme is executed exceptionally well, it is often difficult for the audience to articulate it. (Can you articulate, off the top of your head, the theme of great musical compositions such as Aaron Copland's *Rodeo* or Gustave Holst's *The Planets*?) However, it's important to note this difficulty for us as readers or viewers arises from the *seamlessness* of the story's themes. It rarely, if ever, arises from *the author's ignorance* of those themes.

Regardless whether you are trying to identify theme as the reader/viewer of someone else's stories or as the author of your own story, one of the first places you should look is the ending. The ending always tells you what a story is trying to be about. (Some stories get there organically and successfully; others try to present thematic arguments in their closing scenes that, in fact, are only weakly supported by the preceding story.) However subtle or blatant it may be, the Climactic Moment is the thematic point of the story, with the Resolution scene(s) usually offering some sort of explanatory context.

Once you've nailed down a concrete idea from a story's closing scenes, take a look back through the preceding story. Is that same idea mirrored throughout? If not, it could be the story fails to work thematically. Or it could be you failed to choose the correct concrete definition for the story's abstract theme. In that case, try again.

I have come to define the theme of *The Great Escape* as "the indomitable human spirit." The story ends with most of the escaped POWs either dead or returned to captivity. On the surface, that doesn't seem very indomitable. But two particular scenes prove what the story is about.

One is the response of the senior British officer to James Garner's doubts about the worth of their gambit:

> That depends on your point of view, Hendley.

This suggestion is immediately reinforced by the return of Steve McQueen's character. After facing down the dejected camp commander (who is on his way to a court-martial), McQueen ends the movie with a cocky grin. His defiant strut back to solitary confinement is played against the jaunty but poignant closing score. The scene emphatically underlines the idea that this ending is not to be seen as a defeat.

When this theorized thematic principle is then played back against everything that happens previously in the plot and in the character development, we can see how it resonates in every scene—but in such a subtle way that the power is magnified. The theme is *shown* instead of *told*.

Still, theme remains a slippery thing. A story's thematic premise can often be summed up in more than one way. Some people will look at *The Great Escape* and phrase its thematic premise differently. Usually, however, this variety just offers differing viewpoints of the same principle. For example, one person's "indomitable human spirit" might be another person's "virtuous patriotism."

Thematic principle is the essence of theme. As the central idea which all other interpretations of a story's theme either refer to or evolve from, it is a powerful place from which to begin planning and/or identifying your story's theme.

THE POWER OF THEMATIC METAPHOR IN STORYTELLING

Once you have identified your story's thematic principle, the real work begins. How will you seamlessly join theme to plot? It is your *thematic metaphor* that emerges as the meaning behind your characters' plot adventures in their story world.

Masterful authors create stories that, on their surfaces, may seem to be entirely plot—and yet are very thematic. They do this by convincing readers or viewers to feel and think deeply *without being obvious about it.* The seams with which they connect theme to plot are held together with invisible threads of highly sophisticated metaphor.

The metaphor is one of the most utilitarian techniques in a writer's tool bag. We use it most simply in basic sentence constructions when describing via comparison (such as comparing a writer's skill set to a "tool bag"). At its most macro (and indeed meta) level, story itself is nothing more than a large-scale metaphor: made-up people going on made-up adventures which create descriptive metaphors for real life.

It's no surprise that somewhere in between the sentence level and the story level, we find yet another repetition of the pattern. This is where we come upon the powerful technique of molding plot into a visual, external metaphor for the story's invisible, internal theme.

This interpretation of story can be applied with varying levels of explicitness.

At one end of the spectrum, **allegories** (such as *The Lion, the Witch, and the Wardrobe* and *Animal Farm*) deliberately present themselves as blatant metaphors (for Christianity and Soviet Russia, respectively).

At the other end, **fact-based or docudrama stories** (such as *The Great Escape* or *I, Claudius*) evoke the metaphorical inference of theme by extrapolating and/or shaping a meaning from actual events. (Let me stop and say that successful stories in this category stand in stark contrast to their unsuccessful brethren, which present factual events but fail to transform plot into story by identifying the thematic metaphor or unifying meaning at the core of those events. As an example, Ron Howard's movie *In the Heart of the Sea* is problematic enough on its own, but especially when compared to the famous epic with which it shares source material—the tremendously metaphoric and thematic *Moby Dick*.)

In between the two extremes, we find any number of varyingly explicit approaches to story-as-metaphor. Most "**tales**," "**yarns**," and "**fables**" (as John Gardner distinguishes them) are immersed in the increasingly deeper waters of non-reality (i.e., fantasy) and therefore increasingly obvious metaphor.

For example, **archetypal fiction**—aka **genre fiction**—is shaped by time-honored metaphors that preconceive the story's most basic themes, even as the specific details of the author's individual handling of the familiar storyforms creates nuance, irony, and sometimes even inversion. The Hero's Journey in action stories and the Happily Ever After at the end of romances both come pre-packaged with a certain amount of inherent thematic metaphor.

I have great admiration for the Japanese movie *Wolf Children* because it is able to blend metaphoric theme with an anti-formulaic story. The story is founded on the high-concept premise of a single mother secretly raising her half-werewolf children. That's a premise that could have taken a dozen different directions, including some very genre choices (action-adventure or romance, chief among them). Instead, the story is a leisurely almost "literary" series of vignettes that vividly show the mother's struggles to protect, provide for, and prepare her children for their adult lives.

This is a story about this particular mother raising these particular children with their very particular werewolf challenges. It is presented in quasi-realistic fashion with little emphasis on the fantasy elements. In short, it's a very straightforward story that doesn't really seem to be about anything more than what it's about.

But by the time the end credits roll, to a poignant "remember when" slideshow of the children growing up, it becomes clear that what viewers have just seen is a deeply wrought metaphor for parenthood. We realize the whole werewolf premise was a metaphor for the strangeness and often seemingly insurmountable challenges all parents face in rearing their children.

THREE QUESTIONS TO FIND YOUR BEST THEMATIC METAPHOR

Your first inkling about a story might be thematic. When this happens, you have the advantage of shaping the plot as a metaphor for that theme. But more often what comes first is plot and character. This is trickier, because it means you can't so much *construct* your metaphor as *discover* it. You must look within the existing/evolving plot to identify the emerging theme.

This is a delicate process that should remain as organic as possible. Balancing plot, character, and theme is like juggling: you can handle one ball for only a short time before briefly pushing it away in favor of the next ball—and so on, over and over and over again.

You must be careful not to impose theme too heavily upon plot (at the risk of an obvious morality play) or plot too heavily upon theme (at the risk of a contrived and empty thematic argument). Rather, you must carefully examine, weigh, and *feel* both plot and theme to discover what each is telling you about the other.

Most plots offer certain inherent themes. It's your job to discover what metaphor your plot is offering from amidst its characters' entertaining adventures. All you have to do is ask the right questions.

Here are three to get you started.

1. What Does This Story Look Like From Afar?

It's easy to get mentally buried under all the minutiae of even a brand-new story idea. The characters. The relationships. The action. Individual scenes. Even the character arcs.

All these things are just chips of glittering glass in the overall mosaic of your story. In order to truly see what you have, you must step way, way back.

Up close, the sinking of the *Essex* in 1820 seems to be about nothing more than a rogue whale taking out a whaling ship. *In the Heart of the Sea* certainly couldn't find any greater meaning than that (or at least not one it was able to cohesively portray). Herman Melville, writing about the same events, stepped back far enough to see something else—which he transformed into a ferociously enduring metaphor about man's obsessive search for and battle against God, fate, and the meaning of life.

Although great dialogue, interesting characters, and entertaining scenes are important, don't lose sight of the fact that they're just the trees in your forest. The forest itself is the story. Only in viewing the entire forest can you identify (and then verify) what theme is emerging.

2. Does Your Story Have a Shape?

In considering what theme your plot might evoke, try to analyze your story's many parts for emergent patterns. Stop seeing stars and start seeing constellations. The more you add to your plot, and the more actions your characters perform in the story, the more you should start seeing patterns.

This is how we find endless thematic variety even in genre stories. Romance stories are always about falling in love. But it's only from the particular patterns of each book's characters and their actions that we find each book's specific themes. *Jane Eyre* is not *Pride & Prejudice* and *To All the Boys I've Loved Before* is not *The Fault in Our Stars*. This is true even for different stories within the same series. Whatever the series' overarching theme may be, each story inevitably offers its own private theme, based on its specific events.

Start by looking at your cast of characters. What do they have in common? Don't just look for areas or traits in which they are similar; look for those in which they are diametrically opposite, since these areas actually offer more commonality than not.

From there, look at the characters' relationships. What challenges are cropping up repeatedly, either in comparison or contrast to one another?

Then start looking at your individual scenes and story events. What patterns are emerging? Are you seeing an overall shape? Are the majority of your story pieces pointing toward a deeper internal meaning?

If not, that's okay. It could be there isn't yet enough happening in your novel to reveal any patterns. Or it could be you need to do a little careful pruning to eliminate the meaningless and enhance the meaningful.

3. What Does Your Story Look Like When Stripped to Bare Essentials?

This is an extremely important question—but also a tricky one. It's kind of like asking, "If there was no story, what would the story be about?"

Fortunately, you don't have to go that far. Rather, the point of the exercise is to strip away window dressing. Remove your story's fancy clothing, wigs, makeup until you get down to the flesh. And then you want to see past the flesh itself to nothing but the skeleton.

What does your story's skeleton look like without any distracting coverings?

Your story's structure is the best place to start. Consider all the major plot points. What do they say this story is really about? Do they all align? Are they all pieces of the same whole, all pointing to a consistent answer to the questions, "What is this story about?" and "What does it mean?"

Then go even further. What are your characters' motivations? Goals? Strengths? Weaknesses? Do they all align? What patterns emerge?

Underneath all the fun fluff, you will find your story's archetypal underpinnings. You will find the universal truths that make this story resonate. At the deepest level, those truths will be vast. But you will also find, built upon the big truths, some smaller ones. Those are the Truths this story is trying to tell, and those are the Truths the plot must exemplify through the metaphor of its own specific patterns and actions.

"Character cannot be developed
in ease and quiet. Only through experience
of trial and suffering can the soul
be strengthened, vision cleared,
ambition inspired, and success achieved."
—Helen Keller

2

USING CHARACTER TO CREATE THEME (AND VICE VERSA)

IF THEME IS a story's soul and plot is its mind, then character is its heart. Character is always and ever the life force of story.

When asked to explain what a particular story is about, some people may respond with a plot answer: "It's about the end of the world."

Others may even respond with a theme answer: "It's about whether it's morally acceptable to save the many at the cost of a few."

But implicit within either answer is *character.*

Indeed, the third possible answer is, of course, straight-up about the characters: "It's about astronauts."

The end of the world and its incumbent moral quandaries are hardly interesting unless people are involved. (Or at least anthropomorphic entities. *Watership Down*, after all, is an extremely engaging apocalypse.) You can't have a proper story without people (characters) doing stuff (plot)—which, together, inevitably comment upon reality (theme).

Together, this trinity mutually generates the text, context, and subtext of storytelling.

The outer conflict, represented by plot, exists on the story's exterior and most visual level. This is the **text.**

The inner conflict, represented by character arc, exists on the story's interior level. This is the **context**. It provides the first layer of commentary on the plot's events. When viewed through the differing contexts of different characters' inner struggles, a plot's text can take on many different meanings.

Finally, the story's theme nestles in the center of the Venn diagram. It may never be seen; it may never be explicitly referenced. But even silent, it creates the **subtext**. Depending on how the other two elements are presented, this subtext may either cohesively support or ironically juxtapose the story's text and context.

In short, it would seem the character's personal relationship with the plot events is what creates the thematic subtext. This is 100% true. But if viewed from another vantage, an aware author can also shape the story in the opposite direction by consciously using theme to *create* character arc.

Effective character arcs are inherently related to thematic presentation. This means all discussions of character arc are really discussions of theme. Character arc is, in itself, a deep and complex subject, which I've explored in my book *Creating Character Arcs* and its companion workbook. For the sake of expediency, this chapter assumes a basic understanding of character-arc principles, but if you need more info, jump to the Appendix at the end of the book, which explains all the important beats of the five main types of character arc.

For now, I want to talk specifically about how theme creates character arc *and/or* character arc creates theme (depending which end of the string the author tugs first). I'm necessarily discussing each of these aspects in partial isolation. In the last chapter, we talked about how to identify your thematic premise; in Chapter 3, we'll talk about manifesting theme in the outer conflict of your story's plot. But each is part of the larger symbiosis. None of these three elements—theme, character, and plot—is created in isolation. Instead, the author must employ what I call the "bob and weave." If you have a notion about what you want your theme to be, you might start by investigating how that could play out in the plot, which might prompt you to start developing suitable characters, which might bring you back to questions of plot—and on and on, back and forth, back and forth. For every little bit you develop theme, you must develop character and plot apace. (We'll talk more about applying the bob and weave in Chapter 9.)

So how can you use theme to create character arc? And how can you use your character's arc to identify and solidify your theme? Following is a five-part checklist that will help you identify the thematic pieces already at play and then use them to harmonize your story into a single unified idea.

1. The Thematic Premise's Explicit Argument

As we talked about in Chapter 1, the essence of your theme will be summed up in its thematic premise. There are many ways this premise might be expressed—everything from a single word to a fully-realized sentence. However, when using the thematic premise to develop character arc, the central tenet you're most interested in is its argument.

Implicit within even the most amoral thematic premise will be a central question. That question is going to produce the heart of your protagonist's character arc. It will drive the protagonist's quest throughout the story. The answer may end up being explicit (as with Dorothy Gale's "there's no place like home"), or it may be deeply implicit (as we talked about previously with *The Great Escape*'s "the human spirit is indomitable"). Either way, the search for this answer will define your protagonist's inner conflict.

For Example:

In Charles Dickens's *A Christmas Carol*, the thematic premise's argument might be turned into the question: "What determines the worth of a life?"

In Charles Portis's *True Grit*, the thematic premise's argument might be turned into the question: "Is justice a personal responsibility?"

In Mario Puzo's *The Godfather*, the thematic premise's argument might be turned into the question: "Does defense of one's family justify all means?"

2. Inner Conflict, Pt. 1: Lie vs. Truth

A story's theme is a posited Truth about life. This Truth may be inherently moral ("what does it mean to be a good person?"), or it may be existential ("what is life all about?"). Either way, the story will indicate that a certain Truth is indeed true.

Necessarily, where there is a proposed Truth, there must also be opposing un-truths—or Lies. And how does a story explore these Truths and Lies? Not, your readers sincerely hope, through lengthy exposition in which they are *told* what's what and what's not. Rather, readers want to be *shown*. They want to see your proposed Truth acted out in a realistic simulation. Whether the proposed Truth can hold up under stressful reality will be "proven" (or disproven) by how well that Truth and its opposing Lies serve your character over the course of the story.

Your story's outer conflict will deal with outer antagonists—people and situations that throw up obstacles between the protagonist and the larger story goal. The inner conflict, however, is ultimately a battleground of the mind, heart, and soul.

No matter what type of arc you're using (Positive Change, Flat, or Negative Change, as discussed in the Appendix), the story's central Truth will be the crucial piece needed for the characters to achieve positive ends. If they resolve their inner conflicts by embracing the Truth, the outer conflict will follow suit. If they cling to the Lie and prove unable to embrace the Truth, their external pursuits will end, at best, in hollow victories.

For Example:

In *A Christmas Carol*, Ebenezer Scrooge overcomes his Lie that "the worth of a life is measured in money" and embraces the Truth that "the worth of a life is measured in charity and goodwill."

WRITING YOUR STORY'S THEME | 37

In *True Grit*, Mattie Ross's steadfast Truth that "a careless attitude about justice will create social anarchy" creates measurable change in the world and characters around her.

In *The Godfather*, Michael Corleone ends by embracing the Lie that "corruption and violence are a justified means to an end."

3. Inner Conflict, Pt. 2: Want vs. Need

If we climb another rung up the story ladder from Abstract Theme toward Concrete Plot, we find the next level in your character arc's development. The story's central inner conflict between Lie and Truth will translate directly into the character's Want and Need.

The Lie is rooted in or is the catalyst for one of the character's central Wants. In Change Arcs, this Lie-driven Want will probably directly influence the character's plot goal. In a Flat Arc, the protagonist will already believe in the story's Truth, but will have to contend with the limited Wants of other characters whose adherence to the central Lie will create external obstacles.

At its broadest, the Need is always the Truth. In other words, what any Lie-believing character Needs is the Truth. But like the Want, the Need will often translate into a literal object, person, or state within the external plot.

For Example:

Scrooge Wants to "make as much money as possible." What he Needs is the love of his fellow human beings.

Mattie's Want of "bringing her father's killer to justice" is in alignment with the Need of the world around her, but is obstructed by the moral apathy of the lawmen she hires to help her.

Michael Wants to protect his criminal family. What he Needs is to leave the life of crime.

The reason Man versus Self is one of the most archetypal storyforms is because *all* stories are rooted in this primal and personal struggle of a character's inner conflict.

A character's conflicts with others or the world itself are almost inevitably reflections and/or projections of this person's inner conflicts—his or her cognitive dissonances, conflicting Wants and Needs, sometimes even conflicting Wants and Wants or conflicting Needs and Needs. In order to find inner peace, a character will have to work through the chatter of the many competing inner voices (some of them accurate, all of them passionate) on the way toward understanding the following:

1. What each voice is saying.

2. What underlying motivation each voice represents.

3. Which motives and desires are healthy and which are not.

4. How to reconcile those that are healthy but still seem mutually contradictory.

5. Letting go of some desires in favor of others.

6. Coming into harmony with all choices.

7. Moving forward in holistic action based on those choices.

Even though that internal progression may be the foremost preoccupation of the author and the character, the internal conflict will likely happen behind the scenes and under the surface of the external plot. The plot reflects/projects the character's inner struggle upon the external world.

You can start by thinking of your character's inner conflict as a dichotomous struggle between the Thing the Character Wants (which is Lie-based) and the Thing the Character Needs (which is Truth-based). This black-and-white dichotomy is helpful for an at-a-glance understanding of your character's inner conflict dynamics. From there, you can find greater nuance by looking a little deeper at what is really going on inside your character.

The Thing Your Character Wants: What Is It Really?

At its simplest, the Thing Your Character Wants is the plot goal. The Want is part of a bigger picture—a desire or goal that existed prior to the specific conflict of your story's Second Act—but it funnels directly into your character's plot goal.

For Example:

Luke Skywalker's Want is to escape his lonely orphaned adolescence and find a life of meaning and purpose in the larger galaxy. In *A New Hope*, this translates to the specifically iterated goal of wanting to "learn the ways of the Force and become a Jedi like my father"—a desire that progresses throughout the trilogy and frames his entire arc.

In any kind of Change Arc, the Want reveals the Lie the Character Believes in action. The Want itself may not be a bad thing (more on that in a bit), but even if it is positive in itself, it represents a negative mindset or motivation. Within the character's inner life, the Lie has created either a hole or a block. It is preventing the character from growing toward health; it may even be actively pushing the character toward mental or moral sickness.

At the root of the Lie and its ambiguous motivations is a Ghost from the character's past—something that created that hole or that block.

For Example:

Luke's Ghost is his orphanhood, particularly the absence of his seemingly heroic father.

Luke's Lie is that to fill this inner hole and be worthy, he must be just like that father. This false belief fuels his impatience and reckless desire for adventure and glory.

Because the Lie and the Want are linked (as are the Need and the Truth—see the following section), the obvious implication is that "the Want is bad."

Sometimes this is true. Sometimes what a character Wants is blatantly destructive and evil. However, even in these situations, it's important to note that the character will rarely see it so clearly. He wouldn't pursue the Want if he didn't believe, on some level, that it was worthy and that the end justified the means. As T.S. Eliot chillingly noted:

> Most of the evil in this world is done by people with good intentions.

At the very least, the character may believe that a "bad" Want represents the best possible outcome (as, for instance, when a woman believes she's safer staying in an abusive relationship rather than leaving).

However, even more often, the Want isn't in itself a bad thing. In fact, the Lie and its resultant motivation may not be obviously destructive either. After all, the reason the character believes the Lie and wants the Want is because he thinks it will make his life better. Rather than recognizing his misconception of reality as part of the problem, he sees it as the answer.

This delusion is only possible if the character himself is either utterly confused *or* if he's caught between two conflicting choices, both of which bring their own benefits and consequences. In the case of the abused woman needing to leave her destructive relationship, there will be good things and bad things about either of her choices—which is why the struggle to choose may be waged down to the very bottom of her soul before it can be completely manifested in her external conflict.

For Example:

Luke's Want and plot goal aren't quantifiably bad or destructive. On the surface, all of his Wants and plot goals are actually quite healthy: wanting to become a Jedi, wanting to join the righteous Rebellion and fight the evil Empire, and wanting to move into a more meaningful life in a broader context.

Don't get confused by the terminology. As a technical term within the theory of character arc, the "Want" specifically references a plot-advancing desire that doesn't (yet) represent a wholly integrated or holistic mindset. But just because the character currently wants the wrong thing or wants it for the wrong reason doesn't mean that thing isn't also something he does in fact Need. The Ghost almost always represents a deep gaping Need, and the character's initial attempts to fulfill that Need are rarely 100% misguided.

The Thing Your Character Needs: What Is It Really?

Whereas the Want is a direct equivalent to the plot goal, the Thing the Character Needs is a direct correlative of the thematic value. Whatever Truth your story is positing about reality, that is the ultimate Thing the Character Needs.

For Example:

Luke's Need is to overcome the fear and anger that tempt him into darkness. He Needs to give up his hubristic desire to fight his way to glory as a means of protecting those he loves. What he learns over the course of the trilogy is that being a Jedi has nothing to do with being "like my father." (Indeed, his father must learn to be more like Luke.) Being a Jedi is about surrendering the need for glory, accomplishment, or even control. He learns these Truths slowly, over the course of the series, climaxing in the moment when he refuses his hate and throws away his lightsaber.

The Need is always available to the character. It is an often simplistic antidote to the character's inner pain and conflict. But the character is confused—usually because the Want realistically seems to offer the correct solution to the problem. Just as often, the character may either push away from the Need or embrace it only halfway because she can't gain the Need without also accepting significant consequences (for instance, in leaving an abusive relationship, a woman might have to leave behind much more than just the abuse—not to mention facing punitive reactions from the abuser).

And yet, no matter how difficult or Pyrrhic it might be to pursue and accept the Need, the character will never achieve health or wholeness without it. Ultimately, what the Need/Truth represents is a resolution of the inner conflict. Embracing the Truth shows the character which of the competing voices in her head is right. With this rightness—with Truth—comes a realignment with reality. When that happens, the character may have to face difficult consequences, but she will instantly be freed from the tremendous burden of fighting reality itself.

For Example:

> Luke's Need is to let go of his fear, anger, and hatred. In choosing to do so, he consciously risks his own life, the lives of his family and friends, and even the success of the Rebellion. As it turns out, his story ends positively, since his choice catalyzes his father's subsequent decision to destroy the Emperor and save his son. However, in a story with a Disillusionment Arc, the choice to embrace the Need and the Truth might, in fact, end negatively with the character facing the full consequences of the choice (e.g., Luke's choice could have led to Han and Leia's deaths and the Rebellion's failure).

Just as the Want is not always quantifiably "bad," the Need is also not quantifiably "good" in the sense that choosing it means everything is suddenly sunshine and roses. If embracing the Need were that simplistic, the character would have no reason not to choose it outright at the beginning of the story.

The only reason any of us obstruct our own progression toward health is because pursuing health is hard. For example, even when you know being out of shape might someday threaten you with heart disease or diabetes, this does not mean the daily grueling sacrifices of exercising and eating right are easy choices. This is true even when your bad choices have direct consequences. Maybe you know eating that donut is going to make you feel crummy about five minutes from now. But saying no to all that yumminess is super-hard, so you eat it anyway.

The same goes for healthy mental and spiritual choices. Doing the right thing doesn't always get you a pat on the back; sometimes it gets you crucified—metaphorically and even literally. Choosing to recognize truths about yourself and the world around you doesn't always make life easier; sometimes it rips off the Band-Aid and makes your psychological wounds start bleeding all over again.

That said, the Need *always* represents the path toward health and recovery. A nuanced presentation of the Need will accurately portray all the reasons the character doesn't embrace it outright. But this does not always mean the character might not also actively *want* the Need. For instance, many people who *need* to lose pounds for health reasons also *want* to.

This is where a character's inner conflict comes into play most powerfully. A conflict between something a character Wants and something she does not (even if she Needs it) can be powerful and compelling. But usually, an even more compelling scenario is that in which the character internally struggles between two competing Wants—or even two competing Needs.

She can't have both. She can only have one. In these cases, the true Need (in its technical character-arc definition) will be the one that serves the greater good. For example, the character might Want to be with her true love. Nothing wrong with that. Indeed, the relationship may represent everything that is good about her. It promises nothing but health and happiness for the future.

But the character also Needs to do the right thing. For example, she Needs to make the big sacrifice and save the world because only she can do what must be done. Or on a smaller scale, maybe doing the right thing means staying faithful to her marriage vows and making sure her children grow up in a stable family environment. If she were to choose the good Want over the better Need, she isn't the only one who will suffer. And she *will* suffer. Choosing a Lie over a Truth is always a recipe for suffering, even if the consequences are delayed.

All of this is important because as you're planning your character's arc and trying to identify the Want, Need, Lie, and Truth, it can be confusing (and limiting) when you feel you have to make the Want and the Lie obviously "bad" and the Need and the Truth obviously "good." Even a good-vs.-evil conflict as obvious as *Star Wars* offers a nuanced view of why a character might simultaneously need the Want and want the Need.

Don't get too caught up in the terminology. Ultimately, a character's inner conflict is always between *two* things the character Wants on at least some level. This is, in turn, mirrored in the outer conflict, which also represents Want versus Want—the protagonist's plot goal versus the antagonist's plot goal.

The more calibrated your approach to the polarities of Want versus Need and Lie versus Truth, the more nuanced your thematic discussion and your presentation of plot and character will be.

4. Inner Conflict Becoming Outer Conflict

Your characters' final choice between what they Want and what they Need will be the externalized metaphor that proves the corresponding choice between the theme's Lie and Truth. Readers will never need to be hit over the head with a "moral of the story" when they can be *shown* a character's wrenching choice between two concrete objects, people, or states of being.

This decision should never come easily. If the posited "right" choice is obviously better than the "wrong" choice, the thematic argument will lack teeth. After all, if the right choice is easy, why would the character experience any inner conflict at all?

This is why the argument between Lie and Truth must truly be an *argument*. If a Truth that posits "murderers are evil" is opposed by the simplistic Lie that "murderers are good," there is no argument. But if the Lie is complex enough to allow the author to explore why a defense lawyer might truly believe her psychopathic client deserves not to be punished, then suddenly, you have an interesting premise that can be played out in the external conflict with extremely high stakes.

For Example:

Scrooge must choose between facing the monumental weight of his wasted life or going to his grave unperturbed.

Mattie must choose between pursuing her father's killer and her own safety.

Michael must choose between living a righteous life or protecting his family by any means.

5. Change Within the Character, Change Within the Plot

The surest way to check whether your theme is in harmony with your characters (and therefore your plot) is to examine what changes within your story. How are the characters—particularly the protagonist—different at the end of the story from how they were at the beginning? If there are no changes, then the story will be fundamentally problematic.

Another problem may arise when the character does change, but not in relation to the thematic premise. This reveals a disconnect at some point in the story. Even if you've attempted to paste a different theme onto the surface of the plot (usually through dialogue), what your story is *really* about is always rooted in the change that occurs in your characters and their world.

When we see theme fully integrated with other story elements, that theme will always be an active force, either working change *upon* the protagonist or worked *by* him upon other characters.

For Example:

Scrooge changes from a miser in the story's beginning to a repentant, joyous, and charitable man in the end.

Mattie has wrought change upon the world around her, bringing an end to her father's murderer and his outlaw gang, as well as inspiring certain actions in the complacent and self-serving lives of the lawmen she encountered on her journey.

Michael changes from a clean-cut young war hero with a legitimate career to a ruthless mafia don.

When theme is a message imposed *upon* a story, the result often feels disconnected or even heavy-handed. But when the author works with the theme via the characters, the story's Truth will arise organically.

Choosing a Protagonist Who Is Thematically Correct

It's important that at some point you analyze the soundness of your story idea by considering whether you have chosen the right protagonist for the right story. Although many metrics may inform this analysis, theme is the best measuring stick.

It usually isn't difficult to choose a protagonist; you just write about whichever character most interests you. If you feel there are additional characters who dramatically impact the plot, you can always throw in their POVs as well (although this should never be done lightly). The most important decision is not that of choosing a protagonist or choosing a plot or even choosing a theme. Rather, the most important calibration you can make is to ensure all three are in alignment.

Before we close out this chapter, let's look more closely at how a few well-chosen questions can help you check whether you've chosen the most thematically powerful character as your protagonist. If you discover your protagonist isn't ideally positioned to both advance the plot and "prove" the theme, these questions can also help you to either identify a better protagonist and/or tweak things to bring your plot, character, and theme into better cooperation.

1. What Does Your Protagonist Bring to This Particular Conflict That No Other Character Does?

If you can switch out your protagonist for another member of the cast without significantly changing either the events of the plot or the thematic intent of the Climax, you can be pretty sure you've got a deadbeat protagonist on your hands.

This is also true if you could mix and match your protagonist for a brand-new character who is (or at least seems to be) completely different. For example, if the heroine of your YA romance is a mousy introvert, but the events of the story wouldn't be much affected if you turned her into an angry biker—then she's two-dimensional and thematically vapid in either case.

The protagonist is the monarch of characters. The title raises this particular character above all others. But there must be a reason for this elevation. The character must prove worthy. This doesn't necessarily mean the character needs to have special powers or mad skills. What it does mean is that the character must have or develop qualities that qualify her interaction with the plot events to represent the thematic meaning of those events.

Examine your primary cast and ask yourself: What distinguishes your protagonist? How will this story change her in ways it will not change the others? How will she drive the plot in ways no one else could? How will other characters be impacted by her in a way that could happen with no other character?

2. Why Is This Conflict Your Protagonist's Plot— And Not Anyone Else's in the Story?

Why is *Star Wars* about Luke and not Han or Leia? Arguably, both Han and Leia are more interesting personalities. Certainly, a story with Leia in the lead could have mirrored many of the same plot beats and revelations as Luke's—since they share Force talents and a parental relationship with the hated antagonist who murdered their surrogate families.

Although a story with Leia in the lead could potentially have been just as interesting, it would *not* have been the same story. The central plot in the original trilogy belongs to Luke because it is naïve, idealistic, farm-boy Luke who starts out as the zero. When the story begins, Leia already seems ten years older than her twin. She's too experienced and worldly to represent the story's underlying thematic arc of the journey from Fool to Master. To try to tell anywhere close to the same story from Leia's POV, you'd have to completely change her personality and start earlier in the timeline.

Han and Leia may have gotten more zippy dialogue than Luke did. But the purity and the power of the Hero's Journey could only have been represented in *this* particular plot by *this* particular protagonist.

More than that, this choice is reinforced structurally throughout the story. Despite the time given to Han and Leia's subplot, the structural backbone of the conflict is always and obviously Luke versus Vader—which ties in perfectly with the thematic throughline of Good versus Evil.

3. What Is Your Protagonist's Greatest Virtue?

Sometimes it can be difficult to determine what specific offering a protagonist-elect brings to the table. If you think about it too hard, the lines blur to the point where it seems as if the story could be told with just as much interest and power from any POV. Fortunately, there are a couple additional questions you can ask to help you understand a proposed protagonist's unique offerings.

The first thing to consider is your protagonist's good qualities. What virtue does this character represent that is not initially present in any other character? Think specifically about the contrast between your protagonist and the rest of the cast in the first half of the story.

Your protagonist may be kind when others are cruel. She may be brave when others are cowardly. She may be smart when others are ignorant. She may cling to hope when all others despair.

It's possible this "virtue" may also encompass a special skill. But skills don't usually represent theme in the same way as virtues. Whatever the virtue, it should not be random. This character's kindness, bravery, intelligence, or hopefulness should prove crucial to the development of the plot—either directly or perhaps ironically.

4. What Is Your Protagonist's Greatest Flaw?

Even more telling is the second question you can ask about your protagonist's moral relationship to the theme: What is her greatest flaw? To maintain thematic continuity, the flaw/weakness is very often the mirror image of the virtue. It is the virtue taken full circle, to its farthest extreme, to the point where it is no longer admirable or helpful.

The virtue of kindness may arise from a painfully conflict-averse character. Physical bravery may mask emotional cowardice. Intelligence may ride side by side with socially destructive arrogance. Hope may be blind.

Most protagonists start out with enough good qualities to endear them to audiences (or at least to stoke interest when juxtaposed against less likable tendencies). But those qualities will rarely start out dialed all the way to ten. Rather, when the virtues are inhibited by a partner flaw, they mutually represent both the possibility and the need for thematic change.

5. How Does This Virtue and This Flaw Directly Influence This Plot—and What Do They Say About Both the Plot and the Protagonist?

In a well-constructed story, the plot will initiate the latent change found in the tension point between the protagonist's specific virtue and flaw.

When the plot is created from actions arising from a specific protagonist's virtues and flaws, you'll never have to wonder if you're choosing a thematically pertinent protagonist. You'll also never have to wonder if your plot and your theme are synergetic. When the protagonist is one who both creates the plot and derives personal meaning from its events, you know you've chosen the right character.

"He that wrestles with us strengthens our nerves and sharpens our skill. Our antagonist is our helper."
—Edmund Burke

3

USING PLOT TO
PROVE THEME

SOMETIMES PLOT AND theme are confused as being basically the same thing. Other times, they're viewed as so distinct they don't even belong in the same discussion.

So which is it?

First questions first. Is plot basically the same thing as theme?

To some degree, the answer is *yes*. Or at least intuitive phrasing often links them.

Let's consider Jane Austen's *Pride & Prejudice*. One way of summing up this novel is as follows:

A poor woman and a rich man improbably fall in love.

Plot or theme?

By now, you probably know the answer. What this premise reveals about *Pride & Prejudice* is plot. How do we know? Because what's described is all *external action*; it tells what happens in the characters' world. Even in a romance or social novel, in which much of the "action" is confined primarily to verbal exchanges or even to just the characters' thoughts and emotions, we know we're dealing with plot when we're dealing with anything that references a linear progression of events or realizations.

Now consider another proposed premise for *Pride & Prejudice*, and tell me if this one is about plot or theme:

> A poor woman and a rich man are able to fall in love only after overcoming their mutual prides and prejudices.

It's both, right?

And this is where we find that inherent link between plot and theme.

Plot and theme are not the same thing. As already discussed, theme is an abstract argument (moral or existential) that proposes a truth about reality. But without plot, theme is nothing but an idea. It's a theory to perhaps be discussed with friends over coffee, but it's not a story.

A *story* is what you get when a theme meets a plot. In our second premise, we see how vital one is to the other. The plot ("falling in love") provides the exterior action that proves (or disproves) the theme's proposed argument ("pride and prejudice are both roadblocks to meaningful relationships"). In turn, the theme provides a *why* to the plot's *how*.

Plot and theme are neither identical nor segregated. Rather, plot joins theme and character as the third and most visible of any of a story's Big Three. Plot is the load-bearer of the partnership. Not only must it produce an experience that is both convincing and entertaining, it must also shoulder the substantial weight of providing characters with the external conflict that will force them to engage with the theme.

PLOT SHOULD ALWAYS BE ABOUT THEME

What's a story about? is an extremely broad question. As we discussed in the previous chapter, the answer any given person provides might be variously plot-, character-, or theme-centric. But as we've also discussed, the *true* answer is always theme.

What this means most practically is that what your plot is about is theme. Plot and theme must be linked at such a granular level that it becomes difficult to describe the specifics of one without at least hinting at the specifics of the other. (Put another way: plot and theme will be linked whether you plan it or not.)

The decisions your characters make and the actions they perform will comment on reality in some way. When characters get away with murder—or fall in love at first sight—or become conscientious objectors—or succumb to alcoholism—their stories will say something about how reality is (or at least how the author thinks it should be).

Your story will say these things whether you plan its message or not, whether you even recognize the message or not. Sometimes these oblivious breathings of our unconscious minds provide the most seamless and powerful themes of all. But even more often, an author's lack of awareness about the plot's message will lead to one or both of two undesirable outcomes:

1. The plot ends up "proving" something the writer never intended.

2. The writer unintentionally proves one thing via the plot, while consciously trying to prove another thing through a pasted-on theme that isn't actually substantiated by the story's events.

The former can arise from the author's over-reliance on plot conventions. Instead of searching out honest answers, the author reaches for the same old familiar stand-by seen in a hundred other shoot-'em-ups or romances. As readers or viewers, we've all experienced these stories—ones that expect us to believe the good guys did the right thing *just* because they're the good guys or that the romantic leads fell deeply and lastingly in love *just* because they're young and hot and had a meet-cute.

In contrast, the latter arises from the author's good intentions but poor understanding of what the story was really about. The author intended one theme, but failed to realize the events created in the plot were actually speaking to another thematic argument altogether. The result is an erratic story that at best presents two different themes. At worst, it fails in its presentation of both.

Creating a fully-formed story with an integrated plot and theme is one of the highest aspirations of any writer. Doing so requires skill, and that skill requires awareness. Following are five crucial questions you can use to gut-check yourself about whether or not you've married your theme to the right plot—and vice versa.

1. Why This Plot? Why This Theme?

Two questions for the price of one—because this is the most important query you can make in examining your story's effectiveness. Why must your character endure *this* particular plot in order to learn *this* particular theme? If there is no obvious connection, then either the plot or the theme is the wrong choice.

2. Does This Plot Facilitate a Character Arc That Proves Your Theme?

Your story inspiration may originate with any of the Big Three, but assuming for the moment that it originated with theme, you need to bring your investigation full circle. The theme must be proven within the character arc (via the Lie/Truth debate at the heart of the character's inner conflict), and that character arc must alternatively *cause* or *be caused by* the plot. For the storyform to work, all three must be linked.

You can, of course, proceed with this same investigation no matter which of the Big Three is your entry point. If you're starting with a plot idea (or if you've already finished your first draft), ask yourself what the events of this plot—and your character's journey through it—is saying about reality.

Or if you're starting with character, you can find the Lie/Truth at the heart of the protagonist's arc, then circle around to find a plot to prove that specific theme.

Very often, when you are struck with an idea for one of the Big Three, you'll get simultaneous ideas for one or both of the remaining two. Just make sure you're not taking any one of them for granted.

3. Can Your Plot's External Conflict Be a Metaphor for the Character's Internal Conflict?

Remember, one of the single best ways to get your head around the further symbiosis of plot and character is to think of the story's external conflict as a metaphor for the inner conflict. For instance, if the character is working through beliefs about pacifism, the appropriate external and visual metaphor for this conflict will very likely be a war (or a century of wars, as in Anton Myrer's *Once an Eagle*).

Or perhaps your character is arcing negatively into the degradation of deeper Lies, as in Emily Brontë's *Wuthering Heights*, in which the antihero Heathcliff spends the second half of the book inflicting upon his enemies a grotesque reconstruction of his own childhood humiliations.

4. How Do the External Changes of Your Plot Catalyze Your Character's Inner Changes?

For a storyform to work properly, the outer and inner conflicts must mirror one another. More than that, they must act upon one another. Every beat of the external plot must create enough inner turmoil that the character's arc inevitably advances. And for every beat in the internal arc, the character's changing mindset and motivation must be turned outward to actively affect the exterior events of the plot. Only through this interweaving of outer and inner causes and effects can a consistent theme be fully realized.

Proper scene structure can be a great aid in harmonizing the inner and outer conflicts. Although the entire structural sequence can apply fully to either the outer conflict or the inner conflict, usually it's helpful to view the first half of the structure (Scene: Goal, Conflict, Disaster) as action in the external conflict, and the second half (Sequel: Reaction, Dilemma, Decision) as the internal reaction that will, in turn, roll back around to impact the external conflict in the next Scene.

(If you're unfamiliar with the idea of scene structure, you

can find a full exploration of the subject in the second half of my book *Structuring Your Novel*.)

5. Have You Vetted the Thematic Pertinence of Every Scene?

A story is the sum of its scenes. In our example of the author who wanted to write one theme but ended up with a plot that proved a different theme altogether, the problem was probably caused less by the overall plot and more by a few individual scenes that got away from the author.

Consider every scene in your story. Just as each and every scene should sequentially advance the plot via its external conflict, each and every scene should also be active in its service to theme. It's not enough to reach the end of your book and ask yourself: *What is this story saying?* You must ask that question of every scene: *What is this scene saying?*

If the scene is saying something tangential to the thematic premise—or worse, at odds with it—you must reevaluate the scene's true effectiveness. Like a mosaic, all your many different scenes must eventually combine to produce a meaningful big picture.

A story that is *about* theme is a story that has found its theme deep within its characters and, in turn, used that theme to create its plot. When an author can pull this off, story's Big Three become integral to each other in a way that offers a powerful and compelling visual metaphor for even the most deeply personal moral quandaries.

THE ANTAGONISTIC FORCE AS A DIRECT CHALLENGE TO THE PROTAGONIST'S RELATIONSHIP TO THE THEME

The antagonist may not be the big-money reason readers pick up a book. But he is ultimately the reason the protagonist either:

a) has a reason to stop wasting her life eating potato chips on the couch

or

b) doesn't just coast through every obstacle with boring ease.

So we gotta give our antagonists some love. For starters, this means crafting them with the same nuance and care we lavish on our protagonists. When you stand up an amazingly dimensional protagonist against a cardboard antagonist, readers will always notice.

The antagonist is the flint to the protagonist's steel, the immovable object to the protagonist's unstoppable force, the destiny to the protagonist's free choice. Apart, they may not even be that interesting. Together—*whammo!* Inciting Event!

But it's not enough to just throw a bad guy and a good guy into the ring together. It's not even enough to dream up an antagonist who happens to be opposed to your protagonist's every move (although that's way better). It's also worth noting that giving the devil his due doesn't mean giving him the spotlight. I feel there's an unfortunate trend these days toward overemphasizing the antagonist at the expense of the protagonist. Enemies-turned-antiheroes and redemptive arcs are all fine and well, but not at the expense of narrative integrity or, for that matter, proper use of character-audience identification.

The only way to get your protagonist and antagonist to sing in harmony is to craft them that way from the beginning. The harmonics in any story arise from theme. Just as your protagonist must be carefully chosen/crafted to suit your theme (or vice versa), so too your antagonist.

There are many ways to approach this union of protagonist, antagonist, and theme (which, ultimately, is just another representation of that trifecta of character, plot, and theme). One of the best ways is to take cues from your protagonist's character arc. If you know how your most important character will be thematically impacted by the events of the plot, then you will be able to holistically figure out how to craft an antagonist who both impacts and is impacted by your protagonist's changes.

Basic Categories of Antagonistic Forces

Usually, I prefer the more inclusive term "antagonistic force," rather than "antagonist," since it doesn't assume the antagonist is human. In this chapter, we'll be talking mostly about antagonists who are characters in their own right so I'm mostly using the term "antagonist," but don't forget the same principles apply, if only symbolically, even in stories that don't offer a personified antagonist.

Before we explore how your protagonist's and antagonist's character arcs might thematically influence each other to create a thematic plot, let's first look at some broad categories of antagonistic forces.

1. Protagonist vs. Society

Here we have a protagonist facing off against not just an individual, but an entire society—usually one that is corrupt in some way. Ralph Ellison's *Invisible Man* (not to be confused with H.G. Wells's book of the same title) and Suzanne Collins's *The Hunger Games* represent this genre. However, even in stories of this epic scope, it's usually best to personify the society in either a specific antagonist (Collins's President Snow) or at least a series of symbolic characters (as in *Invisible Man*).

2. Protagonist vs. Nature

This would be any story in which the protagonist is trying to accomplish something (usually survival) in the face of weather (e.g., a hurricane), an unforgiving setting (e.g., a desert), an animal (e.g., predators), illness (e.g., epidemics—or, technically, zombies), etc. These stories may also introduce a human foe but usually in the role of contagonist* rather than antagonist. More often, the protagonist's personal and thematic arc will interact with this faceless antagonistic force in a more symbolic way—with the force of nature offering an externalization of the character's inner battle. Most stories will be better off putting a human face to larger impersonal antagonists—which is why many war movies present a specific soldier as the "enemy" rather than just the entire opposing army.

These stories are simply more emotionally distant. However, remember the antagonistic force is ultimately nothing more or less than an obstacle between the protagonist and her goal. As such, anything standing in the way of the protagonist's goal *becomes* personal.

3. Protagonist vs. Self

There is no antagonist more personal than oneself. We already know every thematically deep story is a story of the protagonist's inner conflict: *who is he? what does he believe? how will he survive? what will he do?*

Very few plots are *entirely* about the Protagonist vs. Self. Even in stories in which the character's internal conflict is the central focus, the conflict will also be externalized in some symbolic way. It could be the protagonist literally gets in his own way by self-destructively throwing up obstacles to his plot goal. But it could also be the struggle against self is represented on a grander scale by having it mirror a larger, faceless conflict (as in Protagonist vs. Nature or even Society) and/or that the protagonist's inner demons are metaphorically represented by the various people he meets throughout the narrative.

Once you know what inner demons your protagonist is battling, you can look for the right exterior antagonist to symbolize, dramatize, and catalyze that all-important interior

---

*The contagonist is a character who unlike the antagonist may be allied to the protagonist in the overall conflict, but who obstructs the protagonist's progress and causes the protagonist to consider backing out of the battle against the antagonist or choosing the wrong moral path to the end goal.

battle. This is the heart of great climactic encounters—when the protagonist's conflict against himself aligns with his conflict against an exterior opponent. One way or another, he will come to the realization that defeating the exterior antagonist is easy in comparison to the inner foe he's been battling. In realizing that, he harmonizes the two conflicts and in ending one essentially ends both. Just like that, you've found powerful thematic resonance within the conflict.

4. Protagonist vs. Protagonist

Most of the time when we hear "protagonist" and "antagonist," we think "good guy" and "bad guy." But this isn't accurate since the terms "protagonist" and "antagonist" are meant to indicate narrative function rather than moral alignment. It's totally possible to have your protagonist be the most evil person in the story and your antagonist be the most angelic.

This deviation from the idea of "antagonist" as "bad guy" becomes most obvious in stories in which the antagonist is actually more of a co-protagonist. What this really means is that each protagonist creates the obstacles to the other's plot goals. These stories are often great for exploring morally complicated themes. They're also customary in romances, in which the central conflict is relational with both characters being equally important in the climactic decision to be together.

5. Protagonist vs. Antagonist

Finally, we have the classic setup of protagonist versus antagonist. In this type of narrative, the protagonist represents the structural throughline, and as such is the character with whom audiences are intended to identify. The antagonist is the person who stands in opposition to the protagonist after their goals turn out to be mutually exclusive. Almost always, the antagonist's goals will predate the protagonist's. The protagonist is the one who, for whatever reason, decides she must react to the antagonist, either to stop the antagonist

WRITING YOUR STORY'S THEME | 63

from doing something or because the antagonist is the one trying to stop her.

WHY YOUR ANTAGONIST MUST BE CONNECTED TO YOUR PROTAGONIST

Thematically pertinent antagonists are the lynchpin to any successful story. You can write delicious protagonists, snappy dialogue, riveting conflict, and deep themes—and still, your story can fail simply because the antagonist was taken for granted as a leering, two-dimensional bad guy.

Somewhat non-intuitively, the character who provides the entire foundation for a successful story is not the protagonist but the antagonist. This is so because the antagonist is the one who connects the conflict to the theme.

If you're uncertain whether your theme and plot are proper partners for each other, the first question is: *What is the relationship between your protagonist and your antagonist?*

What happens in a story is always personal for your characters. Because a story's exterior conflict exists to help dramatize the protagonist's personal character arc, the plot can never be random. Whether your antagonistic force is a faceless corporation, a serial killer, a bully, a family member, or just a nice little old lady who can't remember to chain up her destructive dog—there must be a reason this force is throwing negative obstacles into the protagonist's life.

If there is no reason—no obvious connection—then the story's realism fades. Worst case scenario, the antagonistic force's lack of connection (and thus the main conflict's lack of connection) to the theme creates an utterly fragmented and emotionally unconvincing final confrontation in the Climax.

I see this quite a bit in romances. The main part of the story is solid: it's about a relationship, which means the two figures in the relationship are, in fact, one another's antagonists—creating and resolving each other's obstacles within the mutual goal of a successful relationship. So far, so good. In fact, this fundamental aspect of romances is an excellent example of how to inextricably unite the antagonist, the conflict, and the theme.

But often the author will feel the need to up the ante by throwing in a suspenseful subplot, in which a minor antagonist threatens one of the main characters. This antagonist is usually off-screen for 90% of the book, rarely if ever interacts with the protagonists, and has little to no connection to the thematic premise. Rather, he exists solely to provide an exciting final obstacle for the characters to overcome. No problem there, either, except this final obstacle—which should be the most pertinent and personal of the entire story—ends up being the most distanced from the underlying theme.

In this section, we're going to explore five ways you can connect your antagonist to your protagonist—and thus, your main conflict—in a thematically pertinent way. After reading through the following list, think about some of your favorite stories. Do the antagonists fit into the following categories? If not, drill deeper to figure out what other connections might link protagonist, antagonist, and theme in a watertight triangle of emotionally compelling logic.

1. Protagonist and Antagonist Positively Connected

When you think of a "meaningful connection" between protagonist and antagonist, the first thing to come to mind might well be the heartrending premise of friend versus friend. This is one of my favorite types of antagonist-driven themes, thanks to its inherent emotional quality.

Great conflicts are based around hard choices—preferably leading to obvious lose-lose situations. These are rife in stories in which both the protagonist and the antagonist are forced to choose between someone they love and their own goals and/or principles. These stories prompt excellent moral questions, along the lines of: *What makes it okay to betray a friend?*

This category can also include relationships that aren't necessarily "positive" on a personal level, but which still bind the protagonist and antagonist in a way generally looked upon as a positive alliance. This applies particularly to family members, even when they dislike each other. Cinderella and her stepmother are a good example. They never like each other, but because of their forced familial bond, Cinderella, at least, feels bound to respect the traditional nature of their relationship—which neatly complicates the thematic argument.

For Example:

- Friends Steve Rogers and Bucky Barnes.
  (*Captain America: The Winter Soldier*)

- Friends Steve Rogers and Tony Stark.
  (*Captain America: Civil War*)

- Adopted son/father Matthew Garth and Tom Dunson.
  (*Red River*)

- Brothers Brendan Conlon and Tommy Conlon.
  (*Warrior*)

2. Protagonist Negatively Connected to Antagonist

Many stories open with the protagonist and antagonist oblivious to each other until the moment their goals bring them into conflict. In these moments (either the Inciting Event or the First Plot Point), something happens that is so dramatic and life-changing these characters cannot walk away from each other.

Because the antagonist is traditionally "bad," it's common for her to be responsible for negatively impacting the protagonist in a way that binds the protagonist to her. This action can span the gamut from the antagonist's lying about the protagonist, winning a job away from him, betraying him on a personal level (as in *Warrior*, in which younger brother Tommy feels his older brother chose their alcoholic father over him and their dying mother), all the way to something truly tragic such as an assault upon the protagonist (as when psychotic bandit Liberty

Valance robs, beats, and leaves for dead James Stewart's idealistic lawyer in John Ford's classic *The Man Who Shot Liberty Valance*) or an assault upon a loved one (hello, *Death Wish* and every revenge story ever).

The point is that the protagonist cannot walk away. The antagonist has changed his life in a negative way. The protagonist may start out the Second Act just wanting to try to put things back to rights, but eventually the story will force him to face down the antagonist in what has now become a very personal fight—even if the stakes are actually much bigger than just the two of them. The awesome thing about this approach is that it forces the interior goal to extrovert into an exterior goal, neatly tying everything together.

For Example:

- William Tavington murders Benjamin Martin's son in the midst of the greater conflict of the American Revolution. (*The Patriot*)

- Liberty Valance leaves Rafe Stoddard for dead in the midst of the greater conflict for western statehood. (*The Man Who Shot Liberty Valance*)

- Wrongful King Vortigen kills off rightful King Arthur's parents and friends in the midst of the greater conflict for peace in Camelot. (*King Arthur: Legend of the Sword*)

3. Antagonist Negatively Connected to Protagonist

Instead of the protagonist being wounded and furious with the antagonist, it could be the antagonist who sees himself as the damaged party and pursues the protagonist single-mindedly.

The key difference is that the protagonist is often (although not always) oblivious to the antagonist's obsession with her. She is either unaware of what she did to upset the antagonist, or she views her action positively, or she is unwittingly the key player in a larger conflict of which she is as yet unaware (as is often the case when the conflict is generational, as in *King Arthur*).

This negative connection between characters can work both ways, since any and all of the categories can overlap. Almost always, there will be a chain of cause and effect. Maybe the antagonist gets hurt first, but he will quickly lash out and make it personal for the protagonist as well.

This category lends itself well to mystery and suspense, since the protagonist will sometimes have to investigate to discover whatever it is she did to upset the antagonist and make herself central to this particular conflict. Protagonists who are "chosen ones" often qualify.

For Example:

- Tony Stark versus [pretty much all of his opponents], as a result of his general oblivion about the damage he leaves in his wake. (Marvel Cinematic Universe)

- Rafe Stoddard versus Liberty Valance, as a result of Rafe's trying to lawfully oppose Liberty's reign of terror in the territory. (*The Man Who Shot Liberty Valance*)

- Arthur versus Vortigen, as a result of Arthur's heritage as "born king" threatening Vortigen's reign. (*King Arthur: Legend of the Sword*)

- Po versus Tai-Lung, as the result of Tai-Lung's envy of Po's status as Dragon Warrior. (*Kung-Fu Panda*)

4. Antagonist As a Mirror for Protagonist

Not all stories will feature protagonist-antagonist relationships in which the characters actually know each other. This can create a huge emotional vacuum within the story. How can the conflict be personal when the relationship isn't? How can the Climax still have deep thematic meaning?

In many stories with "Big Bads," it is logistically impossible to even put the protagonist and the antagonist in the same

room for most of the story. Still, you can keep their relationship front and center by allowing the antagonist to be a
symbolic "mirror" for the protagonist. When the protagonist
is able to see himself even in this faraway bad guy, it prompts
the opportunity for the deep thematic grist of existential questions.

The protagonist gets to ask himself: *Why am I fighting this person? How am I any different or any better? If this person is so much like
me, then mightn't we even be friends instead of enemies?*

The more similarities you can draw between protagonist and
antagonist—personality, methods, goals, backstory, interests,
etc.—the more opportunities you will create to explore the
exterior conflict from within the subtext of the protagonist's
own interior journey.

For Example:

- Tony Stark and Ivan Vanko share similar abilities and
  similar backstories regarding their inventor fathers.
  (*Iron Man 2*)

- Steve Rogers and Johann Schmidt share similar experiences with taking the Super-Soldier Serum. (*Captain America: The First Avenger*)

- Jason Bourne shares an identical past with all the
  Treadstone agents sent after him. (The Bourne Trilogy)

- Captain Jack Aubrey duels it out with a French captain, who "fights like you, Jack." (*Master and Commander:
  The Far Side of the World*)

- Elizabeth Bennet and Fitzwilliam Darcy share many
  personality traits. (*Pride & Prejudice*)

- George Bailey and Old Man Potter share business
  savvy, ambition, and a disdain for Bedford Falls. (*It's
  a Wonderful Life*)

- Arthur and Vortigen share a bloodline and similarly
  ruthless ambition. (*King Arthur: Legend of the Sword*)

5. Protagonist and Antagonist Oppose Each Other Ideologically

The protagonist and the antagonist won't always be opposing each other due to personal goals or injuries. Sometimes, the battle will be about greater ideological ideas. The good guy believes in what's "right," and the bad guy believes in what's "wrong"—and never the twain shall meet.

Most story conflicts come down to this at one point or another, even if the theme is just about school kids eking out a pecking order. Stories about larger issues, such as war and social injustice, are often based entirely around ideology.

It's important to note that ideological opposition isn't enough to float a conflict. As you may have noted, ideological opposition implies no sort of connection between characters whatsoever. For the final conflict between these ideologies to carry emotional weight in the Climax, the antagonistic force needs to be further bound to the protagonist via one of the previous categories.

In my opinion, this is where the recent film adaptation of *Wonder Woman* faltered: Diana's final confrontation with arch-enemy Ares is the weakest section of the story, due primarily to the fact that it is entirely ideological. Diana has no emotional connection to Ares. Were it not for her commitment to her beliefs, she would be able to walk away from him and the war with no personal concerns.

At best, this contributes to simplistic plots and themes. Better ideological conflicts are found in the following examples.

For Example:

- Chris Adams's "That's just the kind of promise you've got to keep" versus Calvera's "Why did you come back? A man like you, a place like this?" (*The Magnificent Seven*)

- Rafe Stoddard's law and order versus Liberty Valance's rule by violence. (*The Man Who Shot Liberty Valance*)

- Lady Eboshi's disregard for the balance of nature versus Ashitaki's respect for it. (*Princess Mononoke*)

Don't create a story about a protagonist. Instead, create a story about a protagonist *and* an antagonist—and the connection between them. This demonstrates a realistic conflict that flows, as well as a plot and theme that are bound integrally and powerfully at every important point in your story.

THE THEMATICALLY APPROPRIATE ANTAGONIST FOR EACH OF THE THREE MAIN TYPES OF STORY

You want the antagonist's plot goal to present a direct challenge to your protagonist's thematic orientation. If your protagonist represents or will come to represent the thematic Truth, then your antagonist should be the thematic avatar of the Lie (or vice versa).

This doesn't always mean the antagonist needs to sit down with the protagonist for an ideological or existential debate. It doesn't even necessarily mean the two need to ever be physically present in the same room. But it does mean the protagonist's character arc should be catalyzed by the obstacles presented by the antagonist in the external plot.

Although there are many variations of character arc your protagonist might undertake in your story, we can group those variations within three broad categories. These categories, in turn, offer guidance about what role your antagonist should play in both your story's plot and particularly its theme. (Remember, if you're unfamiliar with the foundational principles of character arc, see the Appendix at the end of this book.)

1. If Your Protagonist Is Following a Positive-Change Arc...

In a Positive-Change Arc story, the protagonist will start out in a negative relationship to the thematic Truth. This means he will begin the story by resisting or outright rejecting the Truth in favor of an opposing Lie. As a direct result of the events created by the main conflict, the protagonist will be forced to confront the limitations of this Lie and start moving into an understanding and embrace of the Truth.

In response, the antagonist may take one of two thematic stances.

The first possibility will begin with an antagonist who *also* believes and represents the Lie. It may be exactly the same Lie with which the protagonist starts out, or it may be a "bigger" version of the Lie to which the protagonist is initially attracted.

Because of their similar alignment with the Lie, it may be the protagonist and antagonist start out on the same side of the conflict. Even if they represent differing goals, the protagonist will still be attracted to and feel an affinity to the antagonist—since at least in their belief in the Lie they are alike.

However, unlike the protagonist, who begins to see through the Lie in favor of the Truth, the antagonist will not change. By the story's end, the antagonist will come to represent the full consequences of following the Lie and will probably be overcome by the protagonist's new Truth.

The second possibility offers an antagonist who aligns with the Truth, opposes the protagonist's Lie from the beginning, and eventually "breaks" the protagonist with the Truth as a way of helping him recognize the Lie is unsustainable. This type of antagonist is less likely to be morally evil or ambiguous. Often, this type of antagonist is an important relationship character, such as the love interest in a romance (e.g., in order for the protagonist to be with the antagonist, the protagonist must overcome his destructive Lie-based mindset).

2. If Your Protagonist Is Following a Flat Arc...

In a Flat-Arc story, the protagonist does not change her primary thematic viewpoint. Thematically, she represents the Truth (or less often and always tragically the Lie). Because of her own powerful alignment to the theme, she will inspire change in other important characters by the end of the story. She will use her alignment with the theme to advance her plot goals.

Stories such as this, in which the protagonist does not personally change, usually present the thematic argument via opposing ideologies. As such, the antagonist will be equally resilient in representing the opposite side of the argument—the Lie if the protagonist represents the Truth, or vice versa.

In these stories, it is possible for the antagonist to undergo a change arc (either Positive or Negative) as a result of interacting with the protagonist. However, this can sometimes put the antagonist in a role of comparative weakness next to an immovable protagonist. A more powerful thematic argument (and thus story) usually arises when the antagonist is designed to represent the opposite, and equally forceful, side of the theme.

3. If Your Protagonist Is Following a Negative-Change Arc...

Negative-Change Arcs offer more variation. The protagonist may start out in either a positive or negative relationship with the thematic Truth. As in a Positive-Arc story, he may start out already believing the Lie—in which case he will either arc into believing a disillusioning Truth or devolve into an even darker version of the Lie. He may also start out believing in the Truth, only to fall away into a Lie.

In these stories, the antagonist may steadfastly represent the Truth, which will be futilely pitted against the protagonist's Lie in a battle of ideologies. Or the antagonist will represent the Lie and serve to seduce the protagonist to his ultimate demise.

THE 4 QUALIFICATIONS OF THE RIGHT ANTAGONIST FOR YOUR STORY

Who will fill the role of your story's antagonist is never a decision to be taken lightly. The wrong decision could derail your story; the right decision could be the key to making your entire book click. To identify an antagonist who will help you take advantage of every aspect of your story, double-check your choice against this four-part checklist.

1. The Antagonist Directly Opposes the Protagonist in the Plot

Boiled down to the lowest common denominator, an antagonist is nothing more or less than the obstacle between your protagonist and her goal. As such, the *right* antagonist will always be directly opposed to your protagonist. He won't stand off to the side of the road, taunting the protagonist or throwing rocks at her. He'll be the guy right in the middle of the road pointing a gun straight at your protagonist's head and telling her to stand down.

If he's not in the middle of the road, then he's not the main antagonist (and/or whatever is at the end of that road is the wrong goal for your protagonist to be pursuing in the main conflict).

Ask yourself:

- What is your protagonist's main plot goal?
- What is the Thing Your Character Wants?
- What character (or thing) is best suited to get in her way?
- How can this character (or thing) directly oppose your protagonist's scene goal?

2. The Antagonist Directly Opposes the Protagonist Thematically

The antagonist is a central cog in the wheel of your theme. Because he drives the external conflict—which is a visual metaphor for the protagonist's inner conflict—he and the conflict he creates must be directly pertinent to the theme.

Every character within your story should reflect upon some aspect of your theme in one way or another, but the main antagonist must offer a direct commentary on your thematic premise. If he's off chasing some other Lie or Truth—or even just a thematic blank—a crucial part of the thematic equation will be missing from your protagonist's arc.

Alternatively, if the antagonist is not directly opposed to your protagonist in the conflict, then it doesn't matter how thematically pertinent he is. His impact on the story simply won't be as vital, because the protagonist's personal discoveries won't be directly connected to overcoming this external antagonist.

Ask yourself:

- Does the antagonist start out either believing basically the same Lie as the protagonist, *or* believing a Truth contrary to the protagonist's Lie?

- Is this character painfully similar to the protagonist in some ways?

- Is this character an example of either someone the protagonist desperately wants to be, or someone the protagonist desperately wants to *avoid* being (or perhaps already is and hates herself for being)?

- Will this character be able to offer convincing thematic arguments with the potential to seduce the protagonist away from the story's Truth—and, as a result, away from her story goal?

3. The Antagonist Is a Reflection of the Protagonist

As part and parcel of the antagonist's thematic role, he needs to offer a jarring fun-house reflection of the protagonist. He is a representation of the protagonist's dark side—of her Lie. Perhaps he is an omen of the protagonist's future fate, or a consequence of the protagonist's past choices, or a revelation of who the protagonist might have been in a different life.

The antagonist is almost always a "negative impact character," one who influences the protagonist's journey toward the light by forcing her to face the power of the Lie's darkness. The more striking the similarities between these vastly different characters, the more opportunities you'll have to explore and develop your theme.

Ask yourself:

- What character best represents where the protagonist will end up if she takes the wrong path?

- What character best represents where the protagonist wants to end up externally?

- What character shares a similar backstory journey with your protagonist?

What character represents or shares similarities with your protagonist's greatest failures to date?

Note that it's not vital for your antagonist to represent the answer to all of these questions, but he should ideally be able to fulfill at least one of them.

4. The Antagonist Creates Obstacles for the Protagonist From the Start

In order to create and maintain a cohesive overarching narrative within your story, you must first create a cohesive and overarching conflict. That only happens when you position the main antagonist to oppose your protagonist's main goals from page one (even if he doesn't immediately reveal himself).

If your protagonist is opposed by first one antagonist and then another, the consistency of both conflict and theme will suffer from the jerkiness, even if your protagonist maintains a consistent plot goal throughout.

Your protagonist and your antagonist can begin your story knowing nothing about each other and can still obstruct each other from the very beginning in ways they won't understand until later in the story. When the characters (and the readers) look back on your story, they should be able to see the main antagonist was in play from the very beginning in one way or another.

Ask yourself:

- What antagonist will be present in the Climax's final confrontation?

- How can this antagonist be the major opposing force against the protagonist at all of the major structural beats?

- How can this antagonist be set up as an obstacle (or the inevitable potential for an obstacle) from the very first scene?

- How will the protagonist "brush" against this antagonist's power in the Inciting Event?

- How will this antagonist drag your protagonist into the main conflict at the First Plot Point?

Consciously crafting an antagonist whose plot actions are motivated by a thematically appropriate relationship to the story's posited Truth and Lie all but guarantees a solid narrative. By deepening your understanding of your antagonist's relationship to the theme, you can add even more nuance by mirroring your protagonist's character arc with an equally powerful arc from a different perspective.

"I don't need a friend who changes when I change and who nods when I nod; my shadow does that much better."
—Plutarch

4

Using Minor Characters to Develop Theme

RAISE YOUR HAND if you've ever written in a new supporting character just because, hey, somebody had to start that tavern brawl.

Creating delightfully colorful, unexpected, and sometimes just plain convenient minor characters is half the fun of writing. That said, we might all want to now sit on those hands we raised.

The more important your supporting characters, the greater your responsibility to ensure they contribute more than just that first punch to get the conflict going. Once you've properly set up the foundations of your story's thematic presentation (via your protagonist's arc and your antagonist's generation of the plot conflict), your supporting characters are going to provide your greatest opportunity for deepening the complexity, maturity, and subliminal power of your story's thematic premise.

Think of your overall theme as a big mirror smashed on the floor. The biggest chunk of glass is your protagonist. The second biggest is your antagonist. Every other shard represents every other character. They all reflect the theme. They all show a different piece of the big picture.

Naturally, the bigger the piece of glass (the bigger the character's role) the more explicit its relationship to theme should be. But ideally even the walk-on character with no lines can present symbolic opportunities.

Think about it: the character who starts that tavern brawl could be a drunken miner, a bartender, a little girl, a fancy gambler, or the landlady. Even if that's all that character contributes to the story, each choice says something a little different within the context.

If dreaming up thematic significance for each and every supporting character sounds like a lot of work, don't worry. With a little practice, it will become second nature to use thematic criteria to choose and/or groom supporting characters. More than that, it becomes a fun and effective way to create a surprising and dimensional cast.

How Minor Characters Define Theme

A protagonist out there alone on a desert island will be able to discover a theme just fine all by himself. But if your story allows you to supply him with a few key minor characters, you can go ahead and put them to work in helping you build a more coherent and resonant theme.

Let's examine a few tactics.

Emphasize Your Minor Characters' Different Approaches to Theme

Let's say your protagonist's journey will ultimately teach him that *true respect must be earned by what a person does, rather than by how rich he is or how much social standing he has.* Basically, you could sum up your theme as *Respect.*

You could explore any number of aspects of respect and disrespect: *respect of self, respect of superiors, respect of inferiors,* etc.

Your main character will be focused on one specific aspect of respect. But your minor characters could each be dealing with their own respect issues. One character might be trying to respect a difficult authority figure. Another might be fighting personal demons of guilt in order to hang on to her last shreds of self-respect. And another might believe that respect is an illusion and, therefore, might as well be gained by deceiving others.

Allowing each character to approach the subject from a slightly different angle gives you a plethora of material to play with in exploring every aspect of your theme.

Contrast Your Sidekick With Your Protagonist

Archetypally, sidekicks are characters who are almost wholly supportive of your protagonist. They're along for the ride on the same journey as your protagonist, and they're cheering him along in his pursuit of his goals. Your protagonist and his sidekick character(s) will share many similarities.

But they should also share key differences. It's in these differences that your theme emerges. These differences can be good or bad. If your protagonist believes only rich people are worthy of respect, your sidekick might believe "it's what you do that defines you." Or if your protagonist believes respect must be earned, his sidekick might be the one who believes it's all right to lie to others in order to trick them into respecting her.

The contrast between the beliefs and actions of these two allies will bring your theme into clearer focus.

Compare Your Antagonist With Your Protagonist

As we discussed in the last chapter, some of the most important aspects of your story will emerge thanks to the ways in which the antagonist and the protagonist *aren't* so different. In *Writing Screenplays That Sell*, story consultant Michael Hauge notes:

> Theme emerges when the hero's similarity to the nemesis and difference from the reflection [sidekick] are revealed…. A nemesis won't necessarily represent some bad quality that the hero also possesses and has to overcome.

The similarity between hero and nemesis can involve either a positive or negative characteristic and it can be revealed at the beginning … at the end, or anywhere in between. The only rule is to find a similarity.

Your protagonist and your antagonist might both have been kids who felt the sting of the societal disrespect that comes from being poor. As a result, they both believe wealth equals respect. That common ground creates interesting thematic possibilities. Both the temptations your protagonist will be subjected to and the warnings (full of foreshadowing!) about what he could become are rife with thematic subtext.

When you use your supporting characters to illustrate your theme, you not only open up the thematic possibilities, you also allow theme to play out naturally in the story—instead of stating it point-blank and cramming it down readers' throats.

REFINING YOUR SUPPORTING CHARACTERS AND THEME

To help you get a sense of how your supporting characters can play a defining role in strengthening and deepening your story's theme, here are six questions you can use to spot and take advantage of missed opportunities.

1. How Does Each Supporting Character Represent the Theme?

Take a moment to scan your cast. If every character is pertinent to the forward progression of your story's plot, then it's already probable these characters have a strong thematic impact as well. Still, it's easy to miss the forest for the trees. For that matter, thematically vetting supporting characters can be a great way to spot weaknesses in their relation to the plot.

Refer to the question inherent within your story's thematic premise. Is each prominent character asking (or answering) some version of this question?

If your story is about duty, your characters may ask any range of questions from "What is duty?" to "Do I owe duty to a tyrant?" to "Can doing your duty go against your conscience?" to "Am I hiding behind my duty?" to "Am I hiding *from* my duty?"

The more varied the questions, the more opportunities you will have to explore your thematic premise from every angle.

2. Which Supporting Characters Reflect Positively on the Theme and Which Reflect Negatively?

Some characters should argue *for* the thematic Truth; others should argue just as passionately and logically *against* it. (If you at least occasionally find yourself *almost* convinced by your antagonist's arguments, you know you're doing a good job.)

There's little point to having multiple characters represent the same thematic position within the story. Seek as much variety as possible. See if you can create a character who will represent at least each of the following:

- A stalwart, unchanging relationship with the Truth.

- A stalwart, unchanging relationship with the Lie.

- A change arc from Lie to Truth.

- A change arc from Truth to Lie.

3. Which Characters Will Influence Your Protagonist's Relationship to the Theme and Which Will Be Influenced By the Protagonist?

Your protagonist's relationship to the plot and the theme is the structural and symbolic backbone that proves whether or not the whole thing works. Supporting characters only matter to the story insofar as they move the needle on the protagonist's relation to the plot and/or the theme (preferably both).

If we simplify the idea of theme to a question, then the supporting characters will reflect that theme by positing various answers. Some answers may help the protagonist find the ultimate thematic Truth he needs to win or transcend the plot's physical conflict. Other answers may be convincing in their ability to tempt him away from that Truth but ultimately negative in their impact upon the ending.

It may also be that a supporting character is impacted *by* the protagonist as much or more than the protagonist is impacted by the supporting character. Especially when the protagonist is demonstrating a Flat Arc (in which he is largely unchanging in representing the story's thematic Truth throughout), the supporting characters may be the ones most changed by the theme.

4. How Does Each Minor Character's Personal Goal/Conflict Comment Upon the Theme?

It's not enough simply to identify the personal beliefs that align a supporting character with either the Truth or the Lie. You must make sure those personal mindsets are demonstrated (*shown* not *told*) on the scene level in ways that move the plot's needle.

The simplest way to gauge this is to consciously choose your supporting characters' personal goals, first within the plot as a whole, then within each scene.

In the busyness of making sure your protagonist's goal and conflict are happening in each scene, it can be easy to overlook the causal and thematic importance of each and every supporting character's scene goal. Paying attention to supporting characters' scene motivations and desires will not only amp their credibility as dimensional human beings, it will also deepen the holistic complexity of your plot conflict and your thematic argument.

5. How Does Each Supporting Character's Climactic Moment Reflect Your Protagonist's Thematic Climax?

Your protagonist provides both the structural and thematic throughline for your story. It's his Climatic Moment that will end the conflict and "prove" the thematic premise. Your supporting characters are there to *support* that outcome. They should not overshadow the importance of the protagonist in these final moments. (If any character other than the protagonist takes center stage in the Climax, you have to consider whether you've chosen the right protagonist.)

Some of your supporting characters may be present in the actual Climax, but many others will offer their final impact on the plot in earlier scenes. Either way, look for opportunities to end these characters' thematic conversations in ways that snowball into the protagonist's finale.

This might look like any of the following:

- The supporting character actively influences the protagonist in moving toward the thematic end.

- The supporting character is directly influenced by the protagonist's thematic choices in the Climax.

- The supporting character symbolically foreshadows or reflects the protagonist's end, either supportively or ironically.

6. What if a Supporting Character Doesn't Provide a Thematic Reflection?

Now we come to the final important question you can ask about your supporting characters. What if they don't have any relationship with or reflection upon the theme?

First of all, don't panic. Not every character has to comment upon the theme. That character who started that tavern brawl at the beginning of the chapter may not need to offer anything more than the first punch to get the scene rolling. But here are two rules of thumb for judging whether you're missing an opportunity for thematic depth or, in some cases, risking a huge thematic hole:

1. The smaller your cast, the tighter your thematic representation must be.

If your story is *Death of a Salesman* with only a dozen characters, then every character matters. The specificity of every character, within both the plot and the theme, must be drawn sharply. If, however, your story presents the proverbial cast of thousands, you'll have much more room for error.

2. The more important the character, the bigger his or her thematic footprint must be.

Although there may be occasional characters whose impact far outweighs their actual screen time, their importance within the story can usually be judged on the size of their roles. Walk-on characters with no lines clearly land at the bottom of the pecking order, while archetypal allies and enemies command the most influence upon plot and theme. You can get away with colorless and meaningless walk-ons, but the more scenes in which certain characters appear and the more dialogue they speak, the greater their thematic importance will become.

Basically, if a character is moving the plot, that character should be vetted for thematic integrity.

Although not always immediately apparent, supporting characters and theme are made to serve one another. If your supporting cast is solid, that's a good indication you're also executing your theme solidly. And if your theme is progressing nicely, it's probably a good sign you've created a memorable and pertinent cast of supporting characters. Using theme to vet supporting characters (and vice versa) is one of your best tools for pulling off a solid and holistic story.

THEMATICALLY COMPLEX SUPPORTING CHARACTERS

At this point you might be wondering if you must create a complete character arc for every single minor character in your story. The answer is definitely not. Fleshing out an entire character arc for all of them would land somewhere between *that's crazy* and *that will* make *you crazy*. Suffice it that it's overkill.

All you need to create complex supporting characters—no matter how large or small their roles—is to answer five important questions about each of them.

1. What Does This Supporting Character Want?

If you're Dr. Frankenstein and your characters are your little monsters, then this question is the electricity that brings them to life—everyone from your protagonist right on down to the walk-ons.

If you look at your supporting cast, you might find one of two problems:

1. The supporting characters really don't want much of anything.

2. If they do want something, then that desire is either to:
   a. Help the protagonist get what he wants.
   b. Stop the protagonist from getting what he wants.

You can do better than this. When I first asked myself these questions as an outlining exercise, I was a little startled to realize my minor characters' desires fit neatly into one of those two narrow categories. I started going through my supporting cast, name by name, and coming up with a specific desire for each of them. The result? Every single character, the protagonist's relationships with them, the main conflict, and the entire plot instantaneously bounced into a new dimension.

Try it. I guarantee your minor characters will go from inconsequential smiling heads to full-on plot catalysts and genuinely interesting humans.

2. What Is Your Supporting Character's Goal?

It's not enough for your supporting characters to *sit around* wanting something. They need a plan of action for how they're going to obtain their goals. Just as with your protagonist's goal in the main conflict, your minor characters need to discover that the course of good storytelling never did run smooth. They're going to have a really hard time getting what they want. They're going to meet serious resistance. Conflict, baby, conflict.

Want it to get even better? The majority of that resistance should be the result of *other* character's goals—particularly the protagonist's—getting in the way of the supporting character. And vice versa.

Let's say your protagonist is a spaceship pilot whose goal is to go off and save the galaxy. Now let's say she has a mother who loves her and who desperately wants to keep her from harm's way. The mother's goal is to stop her daughter any way she can, even if it means lying to recruitment officers—or maybe even breaking her daughter's hand in the door to "protect" her.

Talk about conflicting goals.

3. What Lie Does Your Supporting Character Believe?

Just like your protagonist, your supporting characters will be less-than-perfect people. Their motivations will be driven by their own complicated and often detrimental perspectives on life.

The fundamental heart of every character arc—however complete or cursory—is the Lie the Character Believes. This is what creates the underlying personal motivation and justification for everything the character desires and does.

Let's return to our overprotective mother from the previous example: her Lie might be that she failed to protect her older son, who has already died in the war, and so she must do anything short of murder to stop her daughter from also dying a hero's death.

Or it could be something much smaller and less injurious. In Charles Dickens's *Little Dorrit*, the protagonist's older sister and brother believe they must "do the family credit" by acting high and mighty in order to somehow make up for the fact that their father has been in debtor's prison for twenty years. This creates a wonderful undercurrent of conflict with the protagonist Amy, since she recognizes the folly of this approach and rejects it as ignoble.

The Lie creates the "starting place" for your supporting character. It's the mark on the wall, showing how tall he is at the beginning of the story. At the story's end, you'll create another mark to contrast the first and show how far the character has advanced (or retreated) over the course of the story. Every prominent supporting character in your story should be different in some way at the end from who he is at the beginning.

4. What Flaw Results From Your Supporting Character's Lie?

Out of belief comes action. It's not enough for your supporting characters to simply *have* a false belief. They must then translate that belief into flawed behavioral patterns. The great screenwriting teacher John Truby delineates two possible categories of flaws:

1. Psychological Flaws
These are interior weaknesses that harm only the character himself.

For Example:

Po believes he has no worth because he sees himself as a fat, smelly slob of a Panda with no innate skills. It "hurts" every day just being himself. (*Kung-Fu Panda*)

2. Moral Flaws
These are exterior weaknesses that harm others.

For Example:

Tai-Lung, the antagonist in *Kung-Fu Panda*, believes he is the only one worthy to be the Dragon Warrior. To prove it, he lays waste to the Valley of Peace and nearly kills his own master.

It's important to note that moral flaws are inevitably extensions of psychological flaws. Arguably, Po's self-revulsion harms others since it keeps him from realizing his true power to protect the Valley. More obviously, Tai-Lung's destruction of others is certainly harmful to not just his own desires but also, inescapably, his psychological well-being.

Your supporting character's flaw will be tied up in her desires and goals, but it can also be a standalone characteristic of its own. Although not as essential as the desire/goal, the flaw can also exist without them. It can be used to bring instant depth to a supporting character with no further exploration required.

After all, which is more interesting: a smiling neighbor lady who compliments your new shoes or a grumpy neighbor lady who sprays you with the hose every time you pass on the sidewalk?

5. What Truth Will Your Supporting Character Discover?

When you think of a "well-rounded" supporting character, what image springs to mind? A circle, maybe? This makes sense, because well-rounded characters must always come full circle. Remember how your character's Lie created a "mark" on the wall at the beginning of the story showing where he started out? That was the setup.

Come the end of this character's participation in the story, you're going to need to pay off that setup. You do that by providing the supporting character a Moment of Truth. He will reach a deep and self-shaking realization about himself, his Lie, his goal, and his flaw. He will react to this realization in one of two ways.

Either he will:

1. Embrace the Truth and reject the Lie—ending on a positive note.

2. Reject the Truth and cling tighter to the Lie—ending on a negative note.

Because your supporting characters' Lies/Truths will be much smaller and less complicated facets of your protagonist's Lie/Truth, their journeys will be correspondingly simpler. You don't have to plot every single beat of the supporting character's evolution. The less prominent the character, the simpler the comparison of his before and after states can be.

For the vast majority of supporting characters, you can get away with hitting just two major beats: the setup, in which you introduce the Lie/flaw/Want/goal, and the payoff, in which you at least hint at the Moment of Truth. The desire/goal/flaw will bring characterizing dimension to even the most cursory roles, while the setup and payoff of Lie/Truth will sketch at least the essence of an additional arc that supports your protagonist's main journey.

USE MINOR CHARACTERS TO FLESH OUT YOUR PROTAGONIST

At the deepest of story levels, the minor characters are there to provide thematic representations of your protagonist's various fates. Since character arc and theme are all about the conflict between a posited Lie and Truth, everything in the story should reflect upon that thematic premise in some way. This includes the minor characters.

In his post "Parallel Characters in *Sunset Boulevard*," screenwriter Matt Bird talks about:

> ...the concept of clones, characters in the hero's life who represent possible outcomes, either as cautionary tales or as potential role models.

In *Story*, Robert McKee says it this way:

> Consider this hypothetical protagonist: He's amusing and optimistic, then morose and cynical; he's compassionate, then cruel; fearless, then fearful. This four-dimensional role needs a cast around him to delineate his contradictions, characters toward whom he can act and react in

different ways at different times and places. These supporting characters must round him out so that his complexity is both consistent and credible.

Even if your story has 1,000 cast members, 996 of those characters are going to be primarily background. They provide context for the four most important characters in a story:

1. The protagonist.

2. The antagonist.

3. The sidekick.

4. The love interest.

The first thing to note is that it's not enough to throw a nominal protagonist, antagonist, sidekick, and love interest into your story. In order for these character types to pull their full weight, they must wholly fulfill their unique thematic roles.

Take a look.

1. The Protagonist Represents the Main Thematic Principle

Readers understand the protagonist is the one who will ultimately prove or disprove the story's main thematic principle. She represents either the right principles that will change the world around her (if she is a Flat-Arc character) or the wrong principles that must be changed in her own life (if she is a Change-Arc character).

2. The Antagonist Represents the Flip Side of the Protagonist's Thematic Principle

Unopposed thematic principles are unproven principles. This is the reason great themes rise out of great conflicts. Great stories examine their themes from every possible angle, honestly exploring every question or argument.

As explored in the previous chapter, the antagonist will offer a counter-argument to the protagonist's position. This argument is not necessarily most effective when directly opposed to the protagonist's. Instead, it is through the antagonist's *similarities* to the protagonist that the most powerful thematic arguments arise. For example, the antagonist may share with the protagonist a belief in either the same means or the same end—and in so doing, proves the dangerous aspects of the protagonist's beliefs.

3. The Sidekick Proves the Value of the Protagonist's Thematic Principle

Like the antagonist, the sidekick, or reflection character, is both alike and different from the protagonist. But unlike the antagonist, the reflection is most important through his *differences* from the protagonist.

This is a character who starts out at least nominally on the protagonist's side, sharing the protagonist's own moral views. But it is this character's differences—his inability to share the protagonist's adherence to or evolution into the story's Truth—that provide a strong argument for why the protagonist must fight through and win her thematic battle.

The beauty of this system is that both the antagonist and reflection characters are complex characters of contrast. The antagonist opposes the protagonist in the plot but shares many compelling similarities with the protagonist. The reflection allies with the protagonist in the plot, but presents many telling differences to the protagonist—traits both good and bad.

4. The Love Interest Acts as an Impact Character

Not every story will feature a love interest, but when present the love interest inevitably functions as an impact character—someone who guides the protagonist. While other archetypal characters provide symbolic catalysts and roadblocks on the protagonist's journey, the love interest acts as a sort of measuring rod for the protagonist's progress (or lack thereof).

The love interest does this by symbolically rewarding (drawing nearer to) or punishing (drawing away from) the protagonist, depending on how aligned the protagonist is with the story's Truth.

This does not mean the love interest is perfect or has a perfect understanding of the Truth. But he or she instinctively provides proof that the protagonist can only earn worthiness via an adherence to the thematic Truth.

**

Although it's possible in a larger cast for more than one character to fit into these archetypal roles, you will keep your thematic presentation at its sharpest by likewise sharply defining these four characters and their relationships to one another. When all four are present, you can be sure you've created a strong, compelling, and moving storyform.

As an easy example, let's consider how Marvel's *Iron Man II* uses its minor characters. Every single one is carefully chosen to reflect upon the protagonist Tony Stark or represent a future fate he may experience—depending on the thematic choices he makes in the story.

Ivan Vanko / Whiplash

The antagonist will always be the most obvious representation of the protagonist. It is his similarities to the protagonist that both tempt the protagonist and warn him away from the Lie.

Vanko and Tony are very similar. Both are genius inventors. Both are the sons of genius inventors (both of whom were involved in creating the ARC reactor). Both are tortured by their pasts with their fathers. Both are intent on "putting things right." Tony could end up as Vanko in the blink of the eye (and, indeed, arguably does by the time *Civil War* rolls around).

Justin Hammer

Here's another antagonist, mirroring still more aspects

of Tony's life. Hammer is also an inventor (although not quite so genius), and like Tony he is the head of a major arms manufacturing company (although not quite so successful). He's a wise guy (although not quite so cool as Tony), he's a jerk (although never lovable like Tony), and a selfish wheeler and dealer (just like Tony).

Hammer is a representation primarily of who Tony used to be: a weapons dealer who had no concern whatsoever for the moral ramifications of his actions. All he cared about was being the top dog whatever the cost and however much of a jerk he had to be to get there.

Natasha Romanov / Black Widow

Iron Man II introduced the perennially popular character of repentant spy Natasha Romanov. She provides foreshadowing for the roles Tony will fill in the future—as a reluctant member of SHIELD and the Avengers. In this film, hers is primarily a surface reflection of outer roles, rather than a representation of the Lie/Truth.

Pepper Potts

At Tony's insistence, his not-quite girlfriend, the ever-dependable Pepper Potts, reluctantly takes over Stark Industries. In doing so, her character represents his status as head of the company and his erstwhile position as CEO. Note how by externalizing this particular role of Tony's, the story is able to transform it into a much more active form of conflict. Now, Tony gets to argue with Pepper (representing the aspect of him that would be a "good" CEO), instead of simply internalizing information and making decisions.

Pepper is also, as the love interest and a mentor of sorts, a representation of the Truth. She is Tony's complete opposite: thoughtful, responsible, dutiful, and kind. She represents the ideal the protagonist is capable of achieving if only he can come fully to grips with the Truth.

James Rhodes / War Machine

Tony's rightfully indignant best friend Rhodey is a two-sided reflection. On the one hand, like Pepper, he represents the ideal toward which Tony is striving: a man who is responsible enough to be entrusted with the War Machine suit—without using it for drunken party tricks.

On the other hand, Rhodey also represents Tony's potential fate if he ever completely surrenders his tech to the government. Rhodey's suit is slaved by Hammer and Vanko, turning it into a mindless weapon that threatens even his friends.

Howard Stark

Finally, we have Tony's dad Howard who appears in flashbacks. Tony's relationship with his brilliant father is complicated and full of wounds—but it is also perhaps the most important projection of Tony's future evolution.

Tony is more similar to his father than to any other character: they're both brilliant and conflicted playboys with poor relational skills. In hating his father, Tony is essentially hating himself. He cannot come to inner peace without first harmonizing this outer manifestation of his inner conflict.

Consider the minor characters in your story. How are they already reflections or representations of your protagonist's various traits, roles, and potential fates? How can you strengthen their thematic relationship to your protagonist to create an even deeper and more powerful weave within your story?

"Theme is ... not the same as message.
A message, by my definition, is
a political statement. It is a principle
that concerns people in a particular situation
and is not universally applicable
to any member of the audience."
—Michael Hauge

5

DIFFERENTIATING THEME
FROM MESSAGE

SHOULD STORIES OFFER messages? Common wisdom insists fiction is meant to entertain, not preach. The novel isn't a soapbox for religious, political, social, or philosophical views. If you try to use it as such, you're likely to sacrifice your stories and alienate your readers. As legendary producer Samuel Goldwyn reportedly quipped:

> If you want to send a message, try Western Union.

Yet, ironically enough, many of the world's greatest and most beloved pieces of literature are stories with blatant moral messages. This is because story as a form is inimitable in its ability to say something about the world without needing to say it directly. That's the entire secret of great art. It always has a message—but you don't always notice. We read to be entertained, but many of us also read to learn, to grow, and to stretch our horizons. We enjoy stories that challenge us and inspire us. This kind of depth is found only in stories that are profoundly honest, and stories can never be honest if authors aren't willing to lay themselves open on the page, to pour out their deepest convictions and most passionate beliefs about the human experience.

As an author, your most powerful gift is your unique and integral view of the world. When you strip fiction down to its essentials, the author's viewpoint is all there is. You may mask it artfully in the colorful garb of diverse characters and impartial dialogue, but if you're unwilling to share your own passionate worldview, you're not giving readers anything more than fluff.

Does this mean you should drag out a soapbox and start haranguing readers into converting to your own viewpoints?

Of course not.

Nothing turns readers off more quickly than a condescending author who preaches at them. Incorporating a message into your stories does not mean spelling out beliefs and arguments. Instead, it's a matter of asking hard questions, choosing strong themes in which you fervently believe, and crafting multidimensional characters who struggle with the gray areas of life along with the rest of us.

Being a novelist isn't about offering answers; it's about asking questions. In *A Writer's Space*, Dr. Eric Maisel poses the kind of questions every writer should be asking:

> Writing is interpretation. You are obliged to offer yours. If you want to say nothing, offend no one, tell a happy little tale, and otherwise act the innocent, that choice is available to you. Just remember that even then you are saying something and that we are watching…. You can play it safe or you can speak your mind. Why venture into the public space of readers and audiences if your goal is to keep your real thoughts private? If you are bothering to write, say what you mean…. Make a list of the issues you are willing to shed some blood over. Read your list over. Are you writing about any of these? If not, why not?

It is a common myth about theme that it must be a story's "moral" or "message." Because theme deals with fundamental truths that inevitably affect human morality, it's easy to assume a story's theme must always be specific and applicable to all readers.

This isn't necessarily a false assumption. As we've discussed, theme is about raising questions and suggesting answers that make people think about how to live more honestly and, even, morally. However, there is a major problem with the assumption that theme should be a didactic message, designed to teach people how to specifically enact a thematic principle in their own lives.

Why is that?

Think about it this way. If you create stories that tell people how to put the theme to work in their own very individual lives, then you're going to have to be writing *story situations* that are experienced by *all* humans. Right away, you can see how such a story must become frustratingly vague (and boring). Worse, amidst all that vagueness, it's pretty hard to hide your moralizing intent.

In middle school, I had to read stories about a group of kids who did generic, kid-like things (mowing the lawn, finding lost money, attending birthday parties). Every story ended with the kids learning some important lesson. The problem, which is still vivid in my adult mind, was that this approach—however well-intended—was more about the story's message than its theme.

The Difference Between Your Story's Theme and Its Message

Let's make this easy:

Theme is a general principle.

Message is a specific example of that theme in action.

(And, yeah, I know I said the limiting factor of a story's message is that it is vague, not specific, but I'll explain that in a sec.)

As we've seen, theme is big stuff. Theme is justice and mercy. Theme is do unto thy neighbor. Theme is joy, peace, and love.

Message, on the other hand, is found in the specific story situations that illustrate the thematic principles. Your message is your story's theme in action.

When your character is working through his character arc, headed away from his Lie and toward the new Truth of the theme, the plot events that act upon him and force him to take action are where we find the message. The very specificity of these story situations (just like those we encounter in real life) means whatever aspect of the overall theme the character is encountering in that moment is probably just a tiny piece of it. In *Dramatica*, Melanie Anne Phillips and Chris Huntley explain:

> ...we know that characters often work not toward the real solution but to a perceived solution. And characters frequently grapple with a problem that is ultimately recognized as only a symptom of the real problem.

If your theme is justice and mercy, then your story's message will probably be something much smaller and more specific to your characters, such as Mattie Ross's "justice is worth having, even if you must chase down your father's murderer at the risk of your own life."

The most important difference to understand about theme and message is that theme is inclusive and message is exclusive. In other words, theme applies to everyone; message applies only to the characters and their specific situation.

In Sam Raimi's *Spider-Man*, the theme is "with great power comes great responsibility," but the message is that responsibility means donning spandex and fighting bad guys. In *Spider-Man 2*, the theme is that we all have the potential to be heroic, but the message is that, in order to be heroic, "you have to be steady" and give up any hope of a normal life.

I think we can all agree "with great power comes great responsibility" is a universal truth. It applies to you and me just as much as it does Spidey. But whatever power we may possess, it's unlikely we're going to exercise our responsibility for it by becoming web-slinging vigilantes. The story's message is too specific to apply to us or other viewers: it's exclusive to people bitten by radioactive spiders.

But the theme? Ah, yes, that's inclusive. It applies to all of us—and that's why audiences resonated so strongly with what might otherwise have been nothing but a story about a human spider in tights.

At the beginning of the chapter, I talked about how the problem with stories that focus on message rather than theme is that they end up too vague. But how does that work if message is *more* specific than theme?

You can't have a theme without a message, since your message is the vehicle on which your story's theme will reach readers. The problem is when you try to turn your message *into* your theme.

Remember those middle-grade stories I talked about? The message and the theme were exactly the same: Billy found some money, wanted to keep it, then realized the right thing to do would be to find the owner and give it back. It's a message that applies to kids everywhere, not just Billy. The message isn't more specific than its theme; it *is* the theme. The result is a message that's too on the nose to avoid moralizing, and a story situation that's too vague to create any real curiosity or interest in readers.

How to Find the Right Message for Your Story's Theme

Chances are your theme will arise out of your message rather than the other way around. Most stories start with their characters stuck in a situation, rather than with a theme that then needs a situation to illustrate it.

Regardless, the two are integrally linked. The theme must create the message—or vice versa. Whatever your story's exclusive message, it must be an illustration of your inclusive theme. When Phillips and Huntley tell us "theme will not be a universal meaning for all things, but a smaller truth pertaining to the proper way of dealing with a particular situation," that "smaller truth" is the message.

For Example:

Secondhand Lions' **theme** is having faith in people. Its **message** is that sometimes it's better to believe one's family because they're worth believing in, rather than because everything they've said is actually true.

Jane Eyre's **theme** is self-worth. Its **message** is that even a once-in-a-lifetime love may have to be sacrificed to keep one's soul free.

The Old Man and the Sea's **theme** is that courage and endurance are their own reward. Its **message** is that trying and failing to bring in a giant swordfish will be more validating than giving up a losing fight.

Only once you've identified your story's message can you use it to bring to life your story's theme in the most powerful, integrated, and subtextual way possible.

How to Create a Complex Moral Argument

If your thematic premise comes across as too simplistic or one-sided, readers will inevitably feel like you've rigged the jury. You're not presenting all the facts about your theme's moral argument, which means you're not trusting readers to make up their own minds.

To avoid this, you must create a moral argument that's two-sided. Undoubtedly, one side is right (or "more" right) than the other in your eyes, but you don't want to weight the scales too heavily. You want to raise questions about *both* sides of the thematic premise.

It's not the author's job to make up the readers' minds. Rather, it's your job to present *all* the facts, so they can make up their own minds.

To do that, you first have to make sure you've created an antagonistic force to represent the "other" side in a way that leaves room for an argument. You'll never create a complex moral argument if the "bad" side is so bad no sane person would ever argue for it.

For example, as John Truby keenly pointed out in his analysis of the Oscar-nominated *Trumbo* (about a blacklisted screenwriter in the 1950s):

[It has an] on the nose script that preaches to the choir. It would seem impossible to come up with a complex moral argument in this story because it's so hard to justify the other side.

Some moral arguments are simply too black and white to allow for a complex exploration. If you feel this is the case with the argument at the heart of your story's main conflict, then you have two options.

Option #1: Find a New Conflict

It's possible the simplistic nature of your main conflict is due to overblown, two-dimensional characters—particularly your protagonist and antagonist, who will be representing the two sides of your moral argument.

If your good guy dresses in white, never does wrong, and never doubts his path—and if your bad guy dresses in black, tortures all his subordinates, and laughs maniacally amidst inopportune monologues—then I'm gonna go out on a limb and guess there is a lot more depth you could be exploring here. Deepen your characters and you'll also deepen your conflict and your theme.

Option #2: Look to a Different Aspect of the Story for the Moral Argument

If the main conflict is just too straightforward to lend itself to a complex moral argument, then make sure you're mining other aspects of your protagonist's journey. If she has no reason to explore doubts inspired by the main conflict, then what *can* she be conflicted about?

How about:

- The methods with which she is trying to achieve the desired end?

- Demons of personal worth or capability?

- Interpersonal conflict pitting her against someone she loves or respects?

A powerful theme is not an answer—it's a question. And questions very often have more than one answer. Truth isn't subjective, but our individual takes on it are, and its applicability in varying situations definitely is. As the Chinese proverb says:

> There are three truths. My truth, your truth, and the truth.

If your purpose in writing a novel is to convince readers of *your* truth, you're probably working in the wrong medium. Better buy a podium or a pulpit (or a blog). If, however, you're interested in sharing your truth *and* raising interesting questions about it, you're in the right place.

Theme is about exploration. But you can't explore unless you're willing to step out of the tour bus and visit some dark places. In other words, you must be willing to look at the exact opposite of your theme's posited Truth and explore it just as earnestly and honestly as if you believed it. For every point you raise to support the thematic premise you've chosen, you'll have to raise an equally honest and probing counterpoint.

Favoritism has no place in a powerful theme. Why? Because readers will sniff it out in a second and instinctively discount your Truth a little bit, both because you're obviously prejudiced in presenting it and because they won't appreciate feeling manipulated.

Some stories will come to you complete with a strong thematic idea. For example, the whole story might be about why lying is bad. Your passion about this Truth is why you're writing this story in the first place. As a result, the idea that you have to explore why lying might *not* be so bad could turn your stomach. Robert McKee points out:

> As a story develops, you must willingly entertain opposite, even repugnant ideas. The finest writers have dialectical, flexible minds that easily shift points of view. They see the positive, the negative, and all shades of irony, seeking the truth of these views honestly and convincingly. This omniscience forces them to become even more creative, more imaginative, and more insightful.

If you're not writing scared, you're not realizing your story's full potential. This is never more true than of theme. Authors can't be complacent. If you're unwilling to explore the dark sides of the truths you profess to believe, then you may want to question how strongly you believe them.

Consider every possible objection even the most virulent readers might raise to your thematic premise. Every one of these objections needs to be raised by your characters—and not just the "bad" characters but the protagonist. Take your protagonist down the dark side of your theme and see what you find. Be brutal. Be honest. You, your characters, and your readers will all emerge on the other side having gained more than mere entertainment. For the rest of your lives, you'll all carry the things you've learned about this powerful theme.

"If a writer of prose knows enough
about what he is writing about
he may omit things that he knows
and the reader, if the writer is writing
truly enough, will have a feeling
of those things as strongly as though
the writer had stated them.
The dignity of movement of an iceberg
is due to only one-eighth of it
being above water."
—Ernest Hemingway

6

DEEPENING YOUR STORY'S SUBTEXT

SOMETIMES THE MOST powerful writing is less about what's said and more about what isn't.

One of the thrills of writing is the author's ability to be "all-knowing" within the scope of the story world. Unlike real life, in which we struggle to understand the opinions, emotions, and needs of those around us, writing gives us the power to understand everything. You always know why your characters react in sometimes unexpected and seemingly irrational ways. You know their histories, and you know their futures. You never have to wonder why they think or act; you just know.

But does that mean you should spill *everything* you know?

Beyond the obvious explanation that readers don't want to know everything (who cares if the bad guy has an ingrown toenail or how the main character's best friend happened to purchase his VW Beetle?), sometimes the secret to punching up a scene, adding layers of meaning, and accurately mimicking reality, is to *leave out* certain details.

Ernest Hemingway was a master of the "iceberg theory." He took the art of subtext to a level of his own, often expunging everything from his narratives but the bare bones and leaving readers to glean facts from characters' actions and dialogue. Although not everyone appreciates Hemingway's sparse style, he was able to create a vibrant sense of immediacy and reality in his stories.

Subtext and subtlety share more than just their first three letters. They are, in fact, interdependent. If you find yourself trying to create subtlety in a scene, what you are actually doing is working with the intricacies of subtext. If you consciously try to enhance your subtext, subtlety becomes your chief utensil.

When writing my portal fantasy *Dreamlander*, I struggled with subtext more than in perhaps any other work. From the beginning, one of my POV characters proved herself inaccessible to everyone—including me. An introvert who masked her emotions, hid her true feelings and fears even from herself, and rarely said more than was absolutely necessary—she refused to cooperate on the page. Other POV characters' scenes rattled out in comparative effortlessness to the literal hours I spent watching the blinking cursor whenever it was this character's turn to speak up.

She didn't want to talk—not to me and not to the other characters—and when she did actually thaw out enough to venture a comment or two, her words were veiled. She rarely said what she meant; she skirted sensitive subjects and refused to hash them out in the open.

As I battled my way through her scenes, I began to notice something. Sometimes what she *wasn't* saying became the focal point for entire scenes. As she and the other characters danced around her fears and her anger, surprising patterns began to emerge, and I began to see facets of her character that, although they had always been there under the surface, I had never really noticed or understood.

Her refusal to speak out demanded serious subtext from her scenes. She allowed me to layer subtlety (of both dialogue and action) into her scenes. She forced me to be more creative and meticulous in *showing* her attitudes and opinions, rather than taking the easy route and sharing these things outright through dialogue or narrative.

It took me half the first draft to fully understand this character, but she also taught me much about subtext. When I first began writing her, I approached her as if the one-eighth of her character above the water was all there was. But her true self floated far below the surface. After a little diving, what I found in this character was no less than the art of iceberging.

THE FIVE STEPS TO CRACKING STORY SUBTEXT'S SECRET CODE

Story subtext often seems like magic simply because, by its very nature, it is the execution of the unexplained.

Like theme, subtext is supposed to be invisible. It lives in the shadowy underworld beneath our words. It's the hooded figure whisking around the dark corners of our stories, the mysterious clockmaker greasing gears behind the scenes, the phantom in our opera.

The very mention of subtext gives me delicious chills. The one thing all my favorite stories have in common is their use of subtext. They're about far more than what they appear to be on the surface. They're stories that invite the reader or viewer into the misty netherworld of the story to ask questions about characters and situations, to fill in blanks, to come to conclusions, and to broaden their experiences.

Good story subtext allows readers to observe and learn about your theme without being schooled. Subtext tells readers the author trusts them to understand the story and the characters without needing to have everything pointed out.

1. Story Subtext Arises From the Space Between Two Known, Fixed Points

This is why story subtext is so often confusing. If it's all about what's not shown, then how can you possibly show it? The answer is simply that subtext only works when it arises from *context*.

If subtext is the shadow behind your story, there must first be figures standing in the sun, casting that shadow. Interesting blank spaces only arise from *shown* elements of the story.

To create subtext, you start by explicitly telling/showing your readers certain things about your characters, plot, or story world. You tell them what they *need* to know (otherwise, you have no story). But you do not explain away the spaces in between.

When readers can see the starting and ending points, they will understand the explicit shape of what you're creating. But because you are resisting the urge to explain everything in between those points, you are allowing them to discover the implicit shape in between.

For Example:

Mike Newell's video-game adaptation *Prince of Persia: The Sands of Time* is nothing more than a simple adventure story, but one of the reasons I enjoy it time after time after time (pun!) is because of the rich character subtext it offers.

The main character Dastan is a street orphan who was adopted as a child by the king. That's fixed point #1.

Then the story skips forward to an adult Dastan's devoted but often strained relationship with his adopted brothers. That's fixed point #2.

What happens in between? Although we are never explicitly told how the brothers feel about each other and why, we don't need the story to condescend to tell us because we can extrapolate for ourselves thanks to the context's clearly fixed points.

2. Story Subtext Must Explicitly Exist Beneath the Surface

The idea that subtext is "what is *not shown*" can lead to the assumption that the subtext is basically nonexistent—a blank space.

But nothing could be further from the truth. Subtext is very explicit. It is very real.

If you think of subtext as Hemingway's "7/8ths of the iceberg under the water," you can see how the invisible bulk of the iceberg absolutely exists. If it is to carry any weight, it *must* exist in the author's intentions and in the story's allusions. Otherwise, there *is* nothing but a blank. The story's verisimilitude will become wobbly and unsatisfying, and readers will realize the author doesn't really know what the story is about or where the characters came from.

Since the whole point of story subtext is that you're not supposed to look at it in the direct light of day, writers often get the feeling *they* should tiptoe around their own stories' subtext, never looking at it.

It's true you're not going to give your *readers* a direct look at your subtext, but *you* must be thoroughly familiar with it. The subtext must exist—the iceberg must be under the water—if the story on top is to have any chance of floating.

Create your story's subtext deliberately. This requires an absolute understanding of your characters' backstories, motivations, and goals, as well as a firm grip on their world.

For Example:

Guillermo del Toro's *Pacific Rim* is one of my favorite movies, largely because its subtext is so rich. Like *Prince of Persia*, it's a simple action flick. But it rises above the genre thanks to its storytellers' rock-solid grasp of everything in their story world.

We sense this post-apocalyptic world, scourged by the alien kaiju monsters, is a rich, interesting, and very real place. We don't learn everything there is to know about it (because that isn't important to the plot). But we see enough fixed points within the context (the black market, the military tech, the cults, the Wall of Life) to understand there is a wealth of subtext under the surface.

Even for viewers who don't visit these possibilities within their imaginations, the sense of a wider world makes the story that much bigger, more authentic, and more meaningful.

3. Story Subtext Must Remain Under the Surface

Once you've created context on the surface and subtext under the surface, that's where they both must stay.

This can be more difficult than it sounds. When you go to all the trouble of creating delicious backstory or worldbuilding, of course you want to share it. You love every detail about your story, and you want to share every one of those details with readers.

You also want to make sure readers *get* the subtext. Sometimes I find myself creating beautifully subtextual scenes—and then ending them with an explicit explanation, either because I want to make *sure* readers get it or even because I love what I've created so much I just want to jump up and down and say, "See! See! Did you see how awesome that was?"

Naturally, I have to go back and delete my sometimes paranoid, sometimes exuberant excesses. I have to trust the subtext to carry itself—which it cannot do if I raise it above the surface into context.

The one exception is important story revelations. Often, you will keep certain aspects of your story (backstory secrets, antagonistic clues, etc.) under the surface for most of the story before revealing them in important scenes that advance the plot.

Resist the urge to explain. It's as simple as that. Get into the habit of avoiding on-the-nose explanations in which you spell things out for readers.

This is especially true of dialogue. Although characters certainly will occasionally say things straight, you should make it a habit to force them into talking around subjects or coming at things sidelong or metaphorically. Whenever you find a character saying exactly what he means, stop and question whether you're spoon-feeding readers information that would be more powerful if it remained under your story's surface. (More on subtext in dialogue in a bit.)

For Example:

Jason Bourne is possibly my all-time favorite character for the simple reason that he is never on the nose. He exists almost entirely within his own subtext. For most of the movie series, he is a mystery even to himself, thanks to his amnesia. We see definite fixed points within his personality and his past, but his near silence forces/allows us to extrapolate his true motivations and feelings.

Were the character ever to sit down with a therapist and start explaining every detail about his experiences and emotions, the subtext would surface, and the character's depth and complexity would fade. It's the great restraint shown in these stories that make them intellectually stimulating and emotionally moving.

4. Story Subtext Is Created by Dichotomy

The best and most interesting story subtext is that which arises from a seeming dichotomy. When the fixed points of your story's context seem like they don't quite align, that immediately sparks readers' curiosity. What might exist between these dichotomous fixed points that explains the mystery? You know you've discovered the potential for story subtext when something in your character's behavior or world makes *you* curious.

Note, however, that subtext cannot arise from an *explicit* question. If you raise an explicit question in your story, readers will always expect an explicit answer. The moment anything becomes explicit, it ceases to be subtext. Instead, these dichotomies must remain implicit questions. These arise when readers are subtly led to believe the truth about a character or a situation is different from how it appears on the surface.

Wordplayer Joe Long e-mailed me:

It's always great when there can be a definite dichotomy between interior and exterior behavior. Truly that's the heart of subtext.

Indeed, this is also the heart of character arc, which means the core of your character's journey can be made all the more powerful through a judicious use of subtext.

Avoid presenting characters and situations as exactly what they are. This can be tricky for you, as the author, since *you* know what's really going on under the surface. Resist the urge to share everything with readers right away. Allow the truth to be a story-long discovery for them.

This is especially valuable in character development. If your character is a good person deep down, great. But you don't necessarily need to spell that out for readers right away. Show them something else. Show them the façade the character presents to the world, and only allow the subtext about his true nature to be revealed through his actions.

For Example:

Supernatural's Dean Winchester is a memorable character largely because he's deeply and endlessly conflicted—and because (at least in the first few seasons) that conflict is allowed to remain largely subtextual. Viewers are shown conflicting truths about him: on the surface he is an irresponsible, obnoxious, alcoholic womanizer, and yet in a seeming paradox he also cares deeply about others, even to the point of brutal self-sacrifice.

The dichotomy raises questions. *Why* is this character this way? What is the internal conflict driving these contradictions? And which of these aspects of his nature is the true aspect?

5. Story Subtext Exists in the Silent Spaces

So far, I've been using movies and TV as examples of story subtext. This is largely because the visual, exterior nature of film allows them to be far more subtextual than written narrative fiction.

Even though all these principles apply in written fiction, it's important to realize you will usually need to spell out more in a book than in a movie. Things that can be implied in a film will leave readers confused if they aren't explained or at least referenced in a book.

However, there is a simple trick for maintaining at least the illusion of subtext within a book. *Cultivate your characters' silence.* Even when the story requires you to explain certain things to readers, resist the temptation to have your *characters* spell everything out to *each other.*

If you were to apply the same subtext-laden dialogue from a movie (in which viewers have no idea what the characters are thinking) in a book (in which at least the narrator's thoughts are on display), you can still achieve almost the same effect of complexity and depth simply by cultivating the subtext of silence between the two characters.

Do not allow characters to tell each other exactly what they're thinking. Whenever you find them spelling things out plainly, step back. Is this information crucial to the advancement of the plot or the readers' understanding of what's going on?

If not, axe it.

If so, take another look. Can you rephrase the explicitness of the dialogue to keep some of that iceberg under the water even while sharing the necessary information?

For Example:

Consider these two excellent examples of authorial restraint in not allowing characters to spell things out to one another.

The first is from *The Book Thief,* Markus Zusak's award-winning Young Adult saga of Nazi Germany. In it, the main character Liesel *thinks* the unequivocal words she wishes to say to her doomed best friend Rudy. Readers understand exactly how she feels. But because she doesn't say the words aloud to Rudy himself, they remain a powerful subtext between them.

As promised, they walked far down the road toward Dachau. They stood in the trees. There were long shapes of light and shade. Pinecones were scattered like cookies.

Thank you, Rudy.

For everything. For helping me off the road, for stopping me...

She said none of it.

The second example is an even simpler one. In Jeff Long's apocalyptic thriller *Year Zero*, readers were with protagonist Nathan Lee in a harrowing scene, where he futilely attempted to flag down an American aircraft carrier off the coast of Alaska. Readers fully understand this context to the following conversation, even though this scene's narrating character, Miranda, does not.

> "She was a pilot in the Navy," Miranda said. "On one of those ships that never came home."
>
> "What ships?"
>
> "You must have heard about them. The mapping and search expeditions. They went out to take stock of the planet, but no one made it home. The satellites pick them up here and there. Ghost ships circling in the ocean. Like the Lost *Dutchman*."
>
> Nathan Lee fell silent. Miranda thought it must have to do with his own loss. He looked haunted.

Nathan Lee could have acknowledged his recognition of the ship with one simple line: "I saw it." Instead, he falls silent, allowing the subtext of his pain to deepen—even though readers know exactly what he is thinking.

Deepening Your Characters' Subtext

Subtext is especially crucial in characterization. Think of it this way: people *are* subtext. The expressions, words, and tones we share with the world are a bare scratching of our surfaces. We are all so much more than what others see. We are hidden desires and motives—unspoken humilities and arrogances—impossible dichotomies, hypocrisies, and paradoxes. Half the time, we don't even understand our own unconscious subtexts. Here are four tips for approaching character subtext in your own fiction.

1. Limit the Number of POVs

Character subtext is much harder to access from within that character's POV, if only because internal narrative necessarily spells out certain facets of a character's being. Often, this is a good thing (it's why we love deep POVs). But limiting the number of narrators allows you more opportunities to explore the non-POV characters' subtext. Were you to get in that character's head, even just once, most of the mystery—and subtext—disappears.

2. Limit the Insights of Your Designated POV Character

Even with a single narrator, a story can ruin its chances for subtext either by allowing that narrator to be too insightful herself or by making her privy to too much information too fast. Let readers interpret certain character behaviors, rather than having the narrator immediately jump in with her own interpretations. This doesn't always work, since readers will rarely appreciate an outright oblivious narrator. But done handily in a realistic way, it opens avenues for a deeper subtext that informs both the secondary characters and the narrator, while also allowing for bigger and more frequent plot reveals.

3. Create Dimensional Characters

The first rule of character subtext is that it must *be* subtext. You can't just leave a character a big fat blank and expect readers to think: *Oooh, so much subtext!*

Remember, subtext is all about hinting at *what's already there but not yet visible*. This means creating characters with dimensions to be discovered.

You can do this, first, by giving the character a complicated and interesting backstory that isn't immediately explained, and, second, by making this character a seemingly dichotomous person—for example, one whose surface aggression immediately paints one picture, which is only slowly contrasted with other, less obvious characteristics.

4. Trust Your Characters

The hardest part of creating excellent subtext is trusting your characters to carry it for you. Your first instinct will probably be to lean into the safety net of explaining things to readers ("And, by the way, in case you missed it, this guy really is nice under all the misunderstood surface obnoxiousness").

Don't fall into this trap. Resist explaining your characters' behaviors—either through their own narratives or someone else's. Give them strong and dynamic choices and actions to perform, then let those actions stand on their own. This is the essence of "show versus tell."

When in doubt, go through your manuscript and cross out every instance of explaining. Does the story still make sense? If not, go back and add the necessary clarifications. But you might be surprised with how little explanation you can get away with—and how much stronger your characters' subtext becomes as a result.

DEEPENING SUBTEXT IN DIALOGUE

Good dialogue needs to check five boxes:

1. Advances the plot.

2. Accurately represents characters.

3. Mimics reality.

4. Entertains.

5. Offers subtext.

These are also pretty much the "levels" by which we master dialogue. When we start out learning to write, our main concern is that the dialogue helps us tell the story. That's the White Belt of Dialogue. Along the way, we start mastering other levels, until finally we arrive at our Black Belt examination: Learning how to write subtext in dialogue.

Think of subtextual dialogue as the secret initiation rite of writing. It opens up a door to a whole new mansion of storytelling possibilities—everything from subtlety to irony to thematic significance. Even better, subtext helps you further refine each of the previous four levels of dialogue.

Following are four rules for deepening your dialogue, using examples from Marvel's *Captain America: The First Avenger* (which is a problematic film on a structural level but watchable mostly thanks to its good dialogue).

Rule #1: Don't Say What You Mean

When writing dialogue, our first impulse is often to spell out exactly what's on the characters' minds: "I'm so mad at you right now!" or "I love you!" or "My backstory is making me so miserable and messed up. Whaaa!" (Don't laugh. It's done all the time.)

Go through every conversation in your manuscript and identify the *point* of each one. What is the one thing the characters are wanting to say? Underline any place where they actually spell it out in on-the-nose dialogue. Now brainstorm a way to say the same thing without saying it—by coming at it sideways, by saying the exact opposite, or by implying it through body language or narrative.

For Example:

One of my favorite dialogue exchanges is the bar scene late in *First Avenger* when Peggy Carter's red dress gets everyone's attention. She walks up to protagonist Steve Rogers and his newly rescued pal Bucky, who immediately starts flirting with her. Steve doesn't say a word. The entire exchange is between Peggy and Bucky—but the subtext is all about what Peggy and Steve really want to say to each other. Instead of an on-the-nose exchange in which Steve says, "Hey, we should be a couple and go out after the war," this little gem is what we get instead:

Peggy [to Steve]: I see your top squad is prepping for duty.

Bucky: You don't like music?

Peggy: I do, actually. I might even, when this is all over, go dancing.

Bucky: Then what are we waiting for?

Peggy: The right partner. [leaves]

Bucky [to Steve]: I'm invisible. I'm turning into you. It's a horrible dream.

Rule #2: Bring Dialogue Full Circle

Say something once and it means exactly what it means. Say it twice and it begins to take on new, even iconic meanings. Snippets of dialogue that can be repeated at crucial junctures can frame the entire story and bring it full circle thematically.

See if you can identify dialogue in the beginning of your story that can initially be taken at face value—and then repeated in another situation where its meaning is doubled thanks to the subtext from the first iteration.

For Example:

First Avenger uses this technique several times, notably with the "right partner" line from the example above. In that scene, Peggy is repeating an earlier statement of Steve's, in which he indicated what he was looking for in a romantic relationship. Her return to the same line of dialogue allows her to provide a direct response to his earlier statement without its being on the nose, as it would have been had she immediately responded in the initial scene.

Other repeated lines are Steve's catch phrase "I could do this all day" (as he's getting the stuffing beat out of him) and his earnest inquiry, "Is this a test?"

Rule #3: Surprise Your Audience

Subtext (and humor) arises from the dichotomy between the expected and the unexpected. When a character responds in a way readers don't expect, the result is both amusing and enlightening.

Look for dialogue exchanges where one character asks another character a straight-up question with an obvious answer. What would happen if you switched out the answer for something less on the nose? Perhaps the second character misunderstands (deliberately or not). Or perhaps he responds sarcastically or ironically. Perhaps he lies. Perhaps he just plain ducks the question because he doesn't want to answer. All these options present interesting possibilities for entertaining dialogue that says more about your characters than most straight-up answers ever could.

For Example:

Steve is a pretty straightforward guy, so this technique isn't used overmuch in this movie. However, his misunderstanding of Howard Stark's "fondue" invitation to Peggy is humorous, while doing double duty in speaking to his romantic interest in her ("So you two...? Do you...? Fondue?"). It's followed up in subsequent scenes that, again, allow the dialogue to be about Steve and Peggy's relationship without actually spelling it out.

We also have the humorous moment when Dr. Erskine, whose accent is obviously German, reacts to Steve's inquiry about his origins by ingenuously responding, "Queens. 73rd Street and Utopia Parkway."

Rule #4: Understatement and Irony

Sometimes when you need a character to be clear about what he's saying, you can still avoid on-the-nose dialogue by employing understatement or irony. When this kind of dialogue is done well, readers always understand exactly what the character means, but they also get a little extra bang for their buck thanks to the subtlety of the delivery.

Look for exchanges where characters make absolute statements ("I'm a three-time world champion." "She dumped me." "This is the best restaurant."). Now brainstorm ways to slant these statements using understatement or irony.

For Example:

Steve's first big (unauthorized) mission has him rescuing captured Allied soldiers from a Hydra base. His clothing and methods immediately mark him as unorthodox. One of the soldiers asks incredulously, "You know what you're doing?" There are two obvious answers to this. Steve could either offer the expected and comforting lie, "Yes." Or he could tell the truth about being a "dancing monkey" with zero combat experience.

Instead, he tells a different truth with a totally different subtextual meaning. He pauses, then says nonchalantly, "Yeah. I knocked out Adolf Hitler over 200 times." It's a delightful bit of irony that speaks to his inexperience without admitting to it, while also slyly referencing his true ability, since the only reason he was knocking out Hitler in the stage show was because he's a one-of-a-kind super soldier. That's four layers of meaning in one simple line.

Words aren't always strong enough to convey the impact of certain emotions. At times, silence speaks louder than words. And surprisingly often, silence (or its equivalent in the form of seemingly mundane dialogue that pulls double duty by communicating far more than the face value of the words themselves) offers blinding insight into characterization.

So how do you know when you're better off telling your chatty characters to stuff a sock in it?

When strong emotions are at play.
"I hate you" just doesn't get the message across as strongly as an icy stare.

When an action communicates more strongly or more succinctly.
Whether that action is something as dynamic as an angry wife throwing a salad at her husband's head, or something subtler, such as her pretending to be so absorbed in cutting the lettuce that she doesn't have time to respond to his entreaties, it's hard to argue with body language.

When dialogue adds nothing important.
If small talk isn't advancing the plot, cut it. On the other hand, if that same small talk is offering insight into the situation at hand (such as the characters' fear of discussing deeper subjects), the very "uselessness" of the dialogue becomes a sort of silence unto itself.

When too much information damages the suspense.
If your characters are spouting off everything they know, it's probably time to clap a hand over their mouths. Characters with secrets are always more interesting. Just make sure you're making the existence of those secrets clear to readers. A character who avoids answering a question or who chooses to change the subject skyrockets the value of what he doesn't say.

When it best serves the character.
Some characters just aren't built to be motormouths. The strong silent type can be a challenge to write, but their taciturn natures give authors the opportunity to make sure every word counts.

Never be afraid of the silence of subtext. Use it to your advantage (as do experienced interviewers) to make characters and readers alike perk up their ears and pay attention.

"Symbolism exists to adorn and enrich,
not to create an artificial sense of profundity."
—Stephen King

7

INCLUDING MEANINGFUL SYMBOLISM

A STORY'S MAIN theme will center around the story's moral premise as set forth in the conflict between the Lie versus the Truth. But there are many other aspects to theme. A story with a primary theme of mercy versus justice may also deal with such disparate topics as love, independence, and change.

That's great. The more interesting themes you can pack into a story, the richer it can be. But the more themes you pack in, the more you increase the chances of a fragmented story that's all over the place. How do you present deep and varied themes without letting them turn your story into a three-ring circus?

The primary answer is to make sure you're choosing themes that are all tying together in some way. A coming-of-age story can very easily offer opportunities to explore love, independence, and change within the context of a tight plot, because all these topics are facets of the same forward progress in the character's arc.

Your first task is to make sure all your mini themes tie back into your main theme. Once you've done that, you then get the opportunity to wield an extra special tool for keeping your theme-packed story as tight and cohesive as possible. That tool is symbolism.

Once you've identified your main theme and all its little satellite themes, look for something you can use to symbolically represent them all. Look to your central plot. What external mechanism is fueling the character's arc, and how can that reflect upon all your themes? Maybe the character is writing a book, maybe she's taking dance lessons, maybe she's rallying to a revolutionary cause. Whatever it is, let it do double, triple, or quadruple duty as a representation of all the many thematic aspects of this character's personal growth.

Symbolism can sometimes be a tough concept to get your head around. How do you come up with the right symbols in the first place? What should they be symbolic *of?* And how do you incorporate them into your story without making them so obvious they lose their symbolic value? Symbolism offers one of the richest opportunities for writers to deepen their themes, beyond merely piquing readers' conscious appreciation and instead speaking right into their emotional and subconscious cores. That's a lot of power.

For example, Charlotte Brontë's classic masterpiece *Jane Eyre* offers a wealth of symbolism. Following are five methods of symbolism Brontë used to enhance every aspect of her story.

Symbolism Type #1: Small Details

You can include symbolism in even the smallest of your story's details. The colors your characters wear. The movies they watch. The pictures they use to decorate their apartments. All of these details offer the opportunity for symbolic resonance.

In the first chapter of Brontë's story, the orphaned Jane Eyre is reading a book called *Bewick's History of British Birds*, which features significantly bleak and desolate descriptions of the English landscape. On the surface, these descriptions have no connection to Jane's world—except of course they do. Brontë could just as easily have given Jane a cheery romance to read. Instead, she used the bleak descriptions to symbolize Jane's bleak life with her cruel aunt.

Symbolism Type #2: Motifs

A motif is a repeated design. In a story, a motif is an element repeated throughout the narrative, often to obvious effect. It can also be used in less conspicuous ways that infiltrate the reader's subconscious with a web of symbolic cohesion.

The concept of orphanhood is prominent throughout *Jane Eyre*, most notably in the main character's own status as a loveless orphan. Indeed, the concept of love and what people do to earn it is central to the entire story. Brontë reinforces the obvious aspects of this motif time and again.

For Example:

Early on, a servant sings a song about an orphan girl.

Adele, the child Jane is hired to look after, is ostensibly an orphan.

When Jane encounters the Rivers family, late in the story, she discovers they are newly orphaned themselves.

Brontë never draws attention to the motif by directly comparing these examples to Jane's own orphaned state. Rather, she simply allows their presence in the story to reinforce the overall effect.

Symbolism Type #3: Metaphors

Motifs can also be metaphors. Indeed, some of the best symbols in literature are visual metaphors for thematic elements. You may use fire to represent a character with a hot temper. Running water may become a symbol for purification. Illness might represent sin or corruption.

The main metaphoric motif in *Jane Eyre* is that of birds as symbols for both captivity and freedom. Brontë uses the bird metaphor throughout the story to symbolize the relativity of every character and setting to this fundamental theme. Small plain birds such as sparrows represent Jane. Birds of prey refer to Rochester, the troubled man with whom Jane falls in love.

And Thornfield Hall—Rochester's prison and Jane's sanctuary—is frequently described in terms of a birdcage.

Strong metaphoric language will often emerge in the writing of a story. While rewriting, see if you can identify any recurring motifs you unconsciously created. Can you strengthen them to better represent your theme? Try to figure out ways to use different aspects of the same motif to describe varying characters.

Symbolism Type #4: Universal Symbols

Some symbols are ingrained so deeply in our social psyche they are used in practically every story. The power of these symbols lies in the fact that they will already have been accepted deep into your readers' subconscious minds. (Their potential weakness, of course, is that their very prevalence can make them seem like clichés.)

Weather is a particularly good example. Thunderstorms are often used as the background for a character's defeat—or as a contrast to a seeming victory. When Jane accepts Rochester's proposal, the lightning that strikes a tree in the garden isn't just a random happening; it's a portent of the dark revelations that will soon sunder their love.

Symbolism Type #5: Hidden Symbolism

Some types of symbolism will be so deeply buried within your story that readers may not recognize them at all. Obviously, the value of hidden symbolism is significantly less than that of other types.

For example, Rochester's horse is named Mesrour. Very few readers will catch the significance of this: Mesrour is the name of the executioner in *Arabian Nights*.

Why name the horse this at all? Or why not call him Blackie? Or Beauty? For starters, both these names would have been a poor use of Symbolism Type #1. "Mesrour," even without explanation, enhances the already dark and mysterious tone of the novel. And for those readers who *do* catch the obscure reference, the foreboding symbolism will only be that much stronger.

Symbolism is a delicate dance, but when choreographed correctly, it can spell the difference between a three-star novel and a five-star novel.

"What moves men of genius,
or rather what inspires their work,
is not new ideas, but their obsession
with the idea that what has already been said
is still not enough."
—Eugene Delacroix

8

CRAFTING THE BEST THEME
FOR YOUR STORY

ONCE YOU'VE FIGURED out a theme at the heart of your story, take a moment to analyze whether this is really the *best* theme for *this* story. Might you get a better, more impactful theme if you were able to tweak your plot and character arc?

You can double-check your story's theme by summarizing it as briefly as possible. Is the theme something general like *justice versus mercy*? Or is it something specific like *better to die a pauper than unloved* (from *A Christmas Carol*)?

Summing up your story's theme gives you a better sense of its relative originality and risk. Does your story's theme leap right out at you? Or do you have to do a little digging to identify it? And when you do find it, does it harmonize your plot and character arcs?

The best themes are both universal and unique. But how does that even work? How can you learn to write themes that say something fresh and new—and yet are resonant to every person on the planet?

We've all read a bazillion romances that told us *love is important* and a bazillion action stories that triumphantly insist *good can defeat evil*. In fact, if you want to talk about a universal theme, let's talk about this one: *There's nothing new under the sun.*

Now, let's try to think of a unique theme. Yep. Right now.

Just sit back for a sec and see how long it takes you to think of a totally original theme. I'll do it too.

...

Well, I got zilch. How about you?

Sure, I came up with what maybe seemed like a few unique *angles*. But underlying the specifics of any idea, there always seems to be some peskily simplistic and universal premise. There's *love, justice, mercy, pain, empowerment, death, hope, despair, deceit, truth, fear,* and *courage*. Guess the Greeks covered it all back in 700 BC. The rest of us might as well pack it up and pack it in. No unique themes left for us to play with!

Fortunately, this is where the balance between *unique* themes and *universal* themes comes into play.

Life itself is universal. That's inescapable. The narrative of life is one we all share, and from it emerges deeply archetypal patterns. The very structure of story and character arc are founded in the personal experiences we all share. The reason these basic structural premises work is because humans resonate with them. If we changed them too drastically, readers would fail to recognize them, fail to empathize with them, and, frankly, fail to care about them.

Archetypes go deeper than just story structure and character arcs. Life and death, parents and children, joy and suffering, mercy and cruelty, hope and despair—these and so many more are the fundamental premises of life itself. To write a story so unique that it avoided all these ideas is not only impossible, but ultimately pointless.

Stories are about our commonality. As readers and viewers we seek solidarity with the characters on the page and the screen and, through them, with their writers. Deep down, what we're looking for in a story experience is not the unique, but in fact the familiar.

This is why themes never get old. I will never tire of the victorious feeling from a story that makes me believe *love conquers all* or *good is stronger than evil*.

Readers do, however, tire of seeing the same themes being

told in the same way by the same story. In short, it isn't archetypal themes, plots, and characters that risk overuse, but rather the ways in which they are combined.

How to Write Unique Themes

The difference between a unique theme and a hackneyed theme has less to do with originality than with execution. To create freshness and vibrancy you don't have to posit something radical. But whatever you posit does have to be radically and honestly personal to you. Tell me *good triumphs over evil* (again), and I may close the book yawning. Tell me *good triumphs over evil* as if your life depends on it—and I'll remember you.

Here are four tips for refining your thematic ideas to find their most passionately and personally unique cores.

1. Look for Your Character's Theme

As we've seen, theme is always rooted in character. Your characters, specifically your protagonist, will show you your theme. Even if you try to tack on another theme, what your story is really about is whatever is at the heart of your character's internal struggle.

This means you can't just dream up some wild and unexpected thematic premise and squirt it onto your story like chocolate sauce on a casserole. You have to start with what you've already got. Look at your protagonist—who she is and what she wants—and look at what she's doing in the plot.

Now look harder.

Let's say you're me and you're writing a historical adventure story called *Wayfarer* (which, it so happens, I did). It's a coming-of-age story about an English kid who gets superpowers and runs around Georgian London figuring out what it means to be the good guy and save the day.

On its surface, that's a story about *good versus evil*, with maybe *growing up* thrown in as a side dish. Or maybe, like Spidey, he's learning that *with great power comes responsibility*. All those ideas are inherent within the story's premise. But there's nothing unique there. More to the point: there's nothing personal there.

So we dig deeper. We look at what specific struggles this character is facing.

- What does he want?
- Why does he want it?
- What is he willing to *selflessly* sacrifice in order to get it?
- What is he willing to *selfishly* sacrifice?
- What will he gain and what will he lose by the story's end?
- How will he have changed?

When asking yourself these questions about your character, the right answers might not be immediately evident. You'll have to recognize and reject most of the obvious answers. In the process, you may find your conception of the character and plot evolving into something deeper right alongside your theme.

2. Look for *Your* Theme

Your characters will give you specific manifestations of the themes that are most pertinent to your plot. But your characters are really just extensions of *you*. To tap into the kind of passionate honesty that creates earnestly unique themes, you must first ask yourself some probing questions.

Boring themes are answers. *Love conquers all.* Yawn. So reframe it as a question: *Does love really conquer all?*

What's a *specific* question you're asking about life *right now*?

Once you find a question to which you honestly don't know the answer, you know you've found an interesting thematic possibility.

Consider the issues that are most on your heart right now. What do you find yourself constantly chewing on? Maybe it's a political or social question, or maybe it's a deeply personal question about yourself or your relationships. Maybe it's a question about an illness or work struggle.

Whatever the case, there's grist for the mill right there. In writing about it honestly, you may even find some of your own answers along the way.

How about a *general* question you feel you're *always* asking about life?

Don't stop with the "little" life questions right there in front of your face. Look up and look out. What are the big questions it seems like you're always asking in one way or another?

One of the themes that crops up again and again in my stories is that of identity. My characters are always asking who they are and what their purpose is. Although I don't deliberately insert this premise into my stories, it's always there because it's central to many of the questions I slowly ponder in the back of my own mind all the time.

What's a virtue you feel is undervalued?

If you're writing a story with a Positive Change Arc and a happy ending, your theme will probably focus on affirming a virtue—*love, courage, justice, mercy, kindness, self-sacrifice.* If so, don't just pick the obvious one—*love* for romance and *courage* for action. Instead, choose one that is important to you and that you feel is either undervalued in the world or underrepresented in fiction.

There's a line I often think about in Marvel's *Captain America: Civil War.*

Cap sincerely tells a frustrated Tony Stark, "I don't mean to make things difficult." To which, Tony gripes ironically, "I know—because you're a very polite person."

It made me realize two reasons why Cap is one of my favorite characters in recent stories:

1. His politeness is actually very unique. Few modern characters—much less action protagonists—are noted for their politeness. It fills a gap most of us probably didn't even realize was there.

2. As a "very polite" person myself, I resonate with him. Since it's a "virtue" I appreciate, I both enjoy sharing the commonality with a character onscreen *and* seeing that

character balance its difficult aspects (e.g., being polite without turning into a pushover with no boundaries).

Make a list of the top five virtues or good qualities you value in others and try to cultivate in yourself. How can you thematically explore the difficulties, downfalls, and rewards of these traits in an honest way?

How about a vice that scares you?

Where there's a virtue, there's a vice. Maybe you're writing a dark story with a Negative Change Arc. Or maybe you just want to explore the downfall of your antagonist. Either way, consider the flip side of your favorite virtues. Which vices get under your skin? Murder, rape, child abuse, substance abuse—those are all big ones. But look at the littler ones too—white lies, verbal insensitivity, maybe even workaholicism.

Look specifically for something that gives you a visceral reaction. If it scares you deep in the pit of your stomach, you know you have to write about it. Or maybe it's just something that irks you and makes you want to lash back at others with some equally unattractive vice of your own.

We all deplore actions that hurt others—from war right on down to graffiti. But don't mount a moral high horse just because it's obvious. Choose a vice that has personal significance for you and use your writing to find out *why*.

3. Ground Familiar Themes in Fresh Milieus

Consider some of the stories you've read lately that just don't have that nice clean fresh smell. The reason for this is probably not because you've already seen this particular character, plot, or theme too many times before—but rather because you've seen *all of them* together too many times before.

Original stories are rarely stories that blare their uniqueness in every aspect. Instead, they're stories that take a fresh look at otherwise familiar elements.

For Example:

Star Wars was famously a new riff on westerns.

The Book Thief is a predictable World War II story that used an unexpected narrator to tell a story about children growing up, not in London or Paris, but in Nazi Germany.

The Princess Bride is an utterly familiar fairy tale told in a completely unfamiliar way.

Arguably, none of the themes in these stories is unique. But the stories themselves feel fresh because the themes are conveyed via unexpected messages and milieus.

Archetypal characters, plots, and themes never grow old. As long as humans are living, loving, fighting, wondering, suffering, laughing, and dying—the fundamental things apply.

But if you find yourself writing a certain type of story that always portrays a certain type of theme, stop and question yourself. Would this theme have something better to say in a different story, a different genre, a different plot? Or conversely would a different theme make everything else about this story absolutely pop?

THE IMPORTANCE OF HONESTY IN WRITING CONVINCING THEMES

As writers, we talk a lot about "being honest," "being vulnerable," "pouring ourselves into our writing," and "not being self-conscious." But what does all that really mean?

Let's begin by asking the obvious question: What *is* honest fiction? Here's my take.

Honest Fiction Is...

1. Truthful Fiction

Nobel Prize-winning author Albert Camus famously said:

Fiction is the lie through which we tell the truth.

Good fiction is always going to be *true* fiction. Honesty in fiction begins by presenting premises, situations, reactions, and ramifications that are true not only because the necessary facts are correct, but also because they resonate with the universal reality of morality. This has nothing to do with characters making prescribed "right" choices and everything to do with presenting the effects and costs of those choices with authenticity and candor.

2. Fiction That Has Nothing to Do With Personal Convictions

Harking back to that same Chinese proverb mentioned previously:

> There are three truths. Your truth, my truth, and the truth.

Honesty in fiction is never about presenting *your* truth. It's about presenting *the* truth by first being true to your *characters'* truths. This means that if your story has you putting words into the mouth of someone whose principles and convictions are antithetical to your own, you must still be able to present that character's ideals in a completely authentic way.

Do you hate your bad guy? If so, you're probably not doing as good a job writing him as you could. To write characters well—to write them honestly—you must be able to put yourself into their skins and brains and understand them so completely, even in their objective reprehensibility, that you can love them even as you love yourself. This absolutely doesn't mean you have to agree with them or promote their actions. But it does mean you have to step away from the subjectivity of your own personal pulpit and instead try to write these characters' subjective perspectives.

3. Personal Fiction

Writers are always being told to "write what you know." That line of advice isn't talking about writing stories based only on your life experiences. What "write what you know" really means is "be honest."

This is where all those encouragements to fight through

your fears and "be vulnerable" in your writing come into play. Being honest in your fiction means digging into your core and finding the part of you that understands and resonates with sometimes uncomfortable, sometimes embarrassing, sometimes downright scary stuff in life.

Being honest and vulnerable doesn't mean you have to tell all your deepest, darkest secrets. But it does mean that when you write about your characters experiencing any kind of emotion—whether it's a "good" emotion or a "bad" emotion—you must be able to tap into that same feeling within yourself and use it to convey your character's similar experience without censorship.

Signs You're Not Being Honest

Writing honest fiction is not something we accomplish just because we believe in it. Honesty in fiction is ridiculously hard work. It only happens when we're actively thinking about it and consciously pursuing it with every word we write.

Part of the reason this is so tricky is that honesty in fiction isn't always the most expedient way to serve the plot, have fun, or entertain readers.

Playwright and screenwriter Donald Margulies noted that sometimes we can unintentionally create a jarring note within our work simply by adding scenes, lines of dialogue, or jokes that are at odds with the honesty of the piece but which we have a hard time deleting because they give us "a personal kind of pleasure." In other words, we're not killing our darlings. He says:

> The thing that I absolutely live by is you have to tell the truth. I know that sounds very simplistic. But I think that ... if you're enjoying yourself too much and if you're intruding too much on a character or the voice of a character, [or] if you find that you're stepping back from that character and that situation and you're commenting on it—you're not doing your job. You need to be as true and as empathic to that moment as possible. You can't be at a remove.

What Honesty in Fiction Feels Like

I want to be honest in my fiction, but I admit it: most of the time, I just write. The character is doing something or saying something and I'm just letting the words pour out without necessarily pausing to check how honest they are. But every once in a while, a scene comes along that demands I dig a little deeper. One of those scenes, irrevocably burned into my memory, is the Midpoint battle scene in my portal fantasy *Dreamlander*. A critique partner had told me the early versions of this scene just weren't cutting it. They were too surface, too bland, too ordinary. I needed to dig deeper.

Instead of starting to write right away, I sat for a few moments and thought. This was a scene in which my protagonist was entering a full-scale battle for the first time. His reaction to this experience was not, in itself, crucial to the story, but realistically this was a life-changing event. It wasn't honest of me to allow him to breeze through the experience without his undergoing some massive reactions.

I asked myself, "If I were the one riding into this battle, what would I be feeling?" The result was, I still think, one of the best scenes I've ever written. My editor loved it, my critique partners loved it. It's the scene, more than any other, that is always mentioned specifically in reviews. I dug deep, I was honest—and it resonated with readers.

Writing teacher Martha Alderson (@plotwhisperer) tweeted:

> Dig for truth in #writing. Often what 1st comes is surface—what you've been taught/picked up from others. Authentic #truth [is] deeper.

My surface instinct with that battle scene in *Dreamlander* was to write the stock action-hero stuff, where the character is tough and awesome and nothing fazes him. But the authentic truth was that he would be overwhelmed by the sensory stimuli to the point that he would be almost at a remove from it—as if he were an observer of his own actions.

I think about that scene often. It remains a reminder and

a challenge for me to always go that extra mile, dig a little deeper, and look beyond the easy surface clichés to find the honest emotional and thematic truth at the heart of all my scenes.

If you're ever worried your fiction may be failing, challenge yourself to search out the thematic truth—big or small—in every scene you write.

"It always comes back to the same necessity: go deep enough and there is
a bedrock of truth, however hard."
—May Sarton

9

WRITING YOUR THEME IN THE FIRST DRAFT

PLOTTING A NOVEL is not a linear process. Particularly in the early brainstorming stages, creating the story will not be a simple progression from Step A to Step B. Your brain wants to bounce all over the place: Step A makes you realize something about Step Z, which makes you realize something about Steps D, M, and U. Only then are you able to return to thinking about Step B.

The novel itself, however, *is* linear. When you start writing Scene A in the first draft, you must follow it up with Scene B. Scene Z just has to wait until you get there.

This is yet another reason a good outlining process can be so creatively liberating. To write a controlled and optimized version of your narrative, you must be able to step back and look at the big picture. You must see everything there is to see about your story and realize how each piece affects all the other pieces.

Although we may often segregate various aspects of story (such as plot, character arc, and theme) in order to better get our heads around them, we must always remember none of them functions alone. Plot depends on character, just as character depends on theme.

This means it's impossible to figure out how to outline any one aspect in isolation. Instead, you have to "bob and weave" from one to the next. As you're figuring out your story's plot, many of the questions you'll be raising will inevitably depend on answers of character and theme—and the same is true in reverse. A plot question may lead you down a lengthy rabbit trail about your character's motivations, which will inevitably be informed by his character arc, which will prompt further questions about where he finds himself at the end of the plot.

Be patient with the process. Take each question as it comes. Don't try to fit the aspects of your story into rigid compartments within your outlining process, but whenever you follow a rabbit trail into one aspect of your story, always bring it full circle to return and answer your original question.

Although the "bob and weave" is a technique you'll use in small ways and large throughout nearly every part of your process, there are three particular areas in which you'll want to consciously put it to use.

1. Weaving Your Plot, Characters, and Theme

All three are important, and each must be woven into the other two if they're to join forces as a cohesive and powerful story. It is, however, difficult to work on all three at the same time. Only once you've worked a little on plot will you understand enough to work a little on character—which, in turn, allows you enough knowledge to start comprehending your theme. And so it goes, piece by piece, throughout the story:

- When you work on your character's external goal (**a plot question**), you must also consider how it is influenced by the Thing He Wants (**a character arc question**), which is, in turn, influenced by the Lie the Character Believes, which stands in opposition to the Truth (**a thematic question**).

- When you work on your story's external conflict between protagonist and antagonist (**a plot question**), you must also consider how this conflict is driven by and/or representing the character's concurrent inner conflict (**a character and theme question**).

- When you work on how your character will demonstrate his changing attitudes over the course of the story (**a character arc question**), you must also consider how this will, in turn, change his outer goals and his responses to the external antagonistic force (**a plot question**).

And on and on. Every time you find yourself asking a plot question, you must follow it up with related character and theme questions (and vice versa). If you aren't working on all three elements in concert, one or more will fall out of sync.

2. Weaving Your Protagonist's Goals and Your Antagonist's Goals

Even in situations in which the protagonist and the antagonist are physically separated for much of the story, they cannot be considered in isolation. Together, their mutually exclusive goals create the conflict, which, in turn, creates the plot.

Think of your protagonist and antagonist as lumberjacks on either side of a two-man crosscut saw. They must be pulling on the same saw—back and forth, back and forth. If either ceases to pull on that saw in turn, the saw ceases to move, and the tree won't fall.

This means the characters' respective plot goals must evolve in harmony with each other:

- When you work on your protagonist's overall plot goal, you must then consider how this will be blocked by your antagonist's overall plot goal.

- When you work on your protagonist's scene goal, you must consider how it will block the antagonist's goals—and, in turn, inspire a defensive or offensive response in the form of a new scene goal for the antagonist.

- When your protagonist is off by herself, making plans, you must also be aware of the plans your antagonist is, in turn, making off by himself.

It's far too easy to come up with a cool battle in which your protagonist is doing awesome things—and then fail to tie it soundly into the plot by connecting it with the cause and effect of the antagonist's previous and subsequent goals and actions. A good generalization of plot is that it is the "give and take between the protagonist and the antagonist." This means you must plan their moves in harmony.

3. Weaving Your POVs/Timelines/Plot Points

Once you have successfully woven all your story's foundational elements, you will also want to consider narrative choices that ride a little closer to the surface. These are more "cosmetic" choices. They do not affect the core of your story; they are, however, the vehicle that carries your story.

These elements include such choices as:

- Which POV will you use to tell each scene?

- If your story includes multiple plotlines or timelines, how will you order their scenes within the story?

- If your story includes multiple plotlines or character arcs, how will you harmonize their respective plot points?

All these choices will influence the order of your scenes, the focus of your scenes, and ultimately the entire flow and force of your narrative.

Making these choices requires a big-picture view of your story:

- When you choose to use a supporting character's POV in one scene, what will this add or take away from your main character's POV in subsequent scenes?

- When you are using multiple plotlines or timelines, how can you order scenes to maintain the best flow of tension and interest? How can you order scenes to best contrast or mirror the events and themes in the alternate plotline?

- When you are creating character arcs for multiple characters, how can you harmonize their important moments of evolution around the main structural plot points? How will these choices affect your selection of POVs?

Shaping a story is an exercise in making optimal decisions. There are rarely *perfect* decisions, but when you consider all your story's pieces as players on a chessboard, you will be better able to understand which pieces must be moved, protected, or sacrificed to create the most pleasing overall effect.

A firm understanding of story theory provides the awareness to perform the bob and weave of moving your story pieces with confidence and precision. That is the true goal in figuring out how to plot a novel—not simply to pile one scene on another until you reach the end, but to craft a thematic storyform that is as solid and powerful as possible.

START BY THINKING ABOUT THE ROLE OF THEME IN YOUR STORY'S CLIMAX

If your theme is a question, then the Climax is the answer. When the story-long conflict comes to a head in the Climax, the result of that final confrontation must provide more than just the external evidence of who won—the protagonist or the antagonist. The result of that conflict must also prove your story's theme.

Consider Stephen King's *Shawshank Redemption*. Andy Dufresne's climactic breakout isn't just about his physical escape from Shawshank Prison. It's also the final proof of the thematic Truth that *hope lets us live through horrible circumstances and emerge triumphant on the other side.*

If Andy fails in his escape, he will not only remain in prison for the rest of his life, but his thematic premise will be proven false and its opposing assertion ("Let me tell you something my friend. Hope is a dangerous thing. Hope can drive a man insane.") will be proven true.

If you're still uncertain of your story's theme (or by extension your protagonist's arc), examine your story's Climax. What happens here? What battle is your protagonist fighting? He's almost certainly going to be in pursuit of some physical goal. He needs to kill the bad guy, win back the girl, steal the Maltese Falcon. But beneath the surface of the physical treasure hunt, there's that deeper thematic reason. His motivation for gaining this thing must be central to the theme.

If he fights this final battle for a reason unconnected to your theme, then your story will fall apart. It may still be a slam-bang finale. It may even be a reasonably entertaining story. But it won't be an intellectually and emotionally stimulating tour de force. Worse, it will be fundamentally sloppy and incoherent on at least a subconscious level.

Of course, creating a thematically sound Climax involves much more than the Climax itself. In order to create a Climax that resonantly *answers* your story's thematic question, you have to build a story that *asks* the right question. This involves not just setting up the question in your story's opening act, via the Lie Your Character Believes, it also means creating a consistent, story-long battle between the Lie and the Truth, with first one and then the other commenting adamantly upon the thematic idea—until finally one is "proven" via its success in the story's Climax.

Here's an easy rule of thumb: ask yourself if your story will end with a positive assertion of your theme. If your story ends with this affirmation of your thematic Truth, then it needs to begin with a negative assertion; the story's beginning must posit that the thematic Truth is false.

For example, *Shawshank Redemption* opens with its main character in the most hopeless of all situations: imprisoned for life for a crime he didn't commit with no chance for appeal.

This negative assertion will then be countered by a positive assertion, then by a negative one, then by a positive one—and so on throughout the story until the final confrontation in the story's Climax when the thematic premise is finally proven once and for all.

This works in reverse for a story that will end by disproving the story's Truth: it will begin with a positive assertion.

How will your story end? Happily or unhappily? How will your protagonist have arced? Will she have overcome her Lie and discovered the Truth? Will she have helped others to find a Truth she already knows? Or will she have fallen away from the Truth and into the Lie?

Within the answers to these questions, you'll find your story's theme. Funnel your story's main conflict into a final confrontation that will drive and be driven by the principle at the heart of your theme.

USING A "TRUTH CHART" TO SOLIDIFY YOUR GRASP OF THEME

The "Truth Chart" is a fast, one-page beat sheet designed to help you get your head around the big picture of theme and character, so you can see at a glance if everything is holding together and progressing realistically.

Thematic Truths (and to a lesser extent Lies) often seem unwieldy in their abstract vastness (especially if the thematic Truth underlying your story is something titanic, like *love*). Because these universal subjects can be accurately expressed in so many ways, they're often difficult to pin down, and over the course of your story, you may find yourself expressing the same core Truth in a dozen different ways. When trying to create a thematically cohesive story, this abstract nature of the subjects with which you're dealing can often be bewildering.

While in the middle of outlining one of my own novels, I found I needed a specific exercise to help me ensure my plot and character arcs were thematically sound at every beat. This practice ended up becoming a tool all its own—the Truth Chart.

What Does a Truth Chart Look Like?

In a minute, we'll define each of the specific parts of the Truth Chart, but first off, here's what it looks like:

Story's Big Truth (Main Theme):
Story's Big Lie:

Character's Specific Truth:
Character's Specific Lie:

The Thing the Character Wants:
The Thing the Character Needs:
The Character's Backstory Ghost:

1st Act—Specific Manifestation of the "Big Lie":
1st Act—The Story's "Small" Introductory Truth:

2nd Act—An Aspect of the Truth Acting as an Antidote to the Specific Lie (Moment of Truth):

3rd Act—Remaining "Biggest" Chunk of the Lie:
3rd Act—Climactic Truth:

Building Your Thematic Truth Chart Line by Line

For explanations of each of these elements and how they should interact within your story, you can refer to the Appendix: "The Five Main Character Arcs" at the end of the book. But for now here's a quick overview of each piece.

Story's Big Truth (Main Theme): This will be your story's thematic premise. It should be a universal principle (e.g., *hope gives people a reason to go on living*) rather than your character's specific Truth (e.g., *hope will help you survive and escape an unjust prison sentence*). It's also best if you can create an intentional statement, rather than just a single-word principle (e.g., *hope*).

Story's Big Lie: This is the Big Lie standing in opposition to the Big Truth. Like the Big Truth, it is a generalized version of the specific Lie the Character Believes. This is the Lie that will affect every part of your story, including supporting characters, the world around the protagonist, and the antagonistic force.

Character's Specific Truth: This is any given character's *specific* version of the Truth, as found in the circumstances of this specific story. For instance, many stories offer a "Big Truth" about, say, *redemptive love*, but the manifestation of your story's specific Truth on this subject can be as vastly different as *Jane Eyre* is from *Logan*.

Character's Specific Lie: The Big Truth (and Big Lie) are positioned at the top of the chart because *that* Truth is your story's defining principle. However, your creative process will more likely discover your story's thematic premise via a specific Lie the Character Believes. This Lie is at the root of the plot problems. The character believes something about himself or the world that is untrue—and his lack of understanding will create consistent obstacles (i.e., conflict) between him and his ultimate plot goal.

The Thing the Character Wants: Although often representative of a larger, more abstract desire (e.g., "to be loved"), the Thing the Character Wants will manifest specifically in his plot goal. Often, the Thing the Character Wants is at least partially misguided, based on the character's mistaken (Lie-based) reasons for wanting it or methods for gaining it.

The Thing the Character Needs: Although the Thing the Character Needs is ultimately an understanding of the Truth, the Need will also usually be represented by a more concrete and specific outer-world objective. Sometimes the character will run away from the Need in the beginning. However, in many stories he may consciously also "want" the Need, which exacerbates the inner conflict between his Lie-based Want and the Truth-based Need.

The Character's Backstory Ghost: The Ghost (sometimes called the Wound) is a motivating event in your character's past that represents the moment and the reason the Lie first took root in his life. Often the Ghost is a traumatic event (e.g., the death of one's parents), but it can also be a "good" occurrence that led to a misunderstanding about life (e.g., receiving lots of praise for one specific accomplishment).

1st Act—Specific Manifestation of the "Big Lie": In the First Act, the story's Big Lie will initially manifest in a specific message that is either urging the protagonist toward the Want and/or presenting a direct obstacle to the protagonist's ability to move forward toward the Need and/or the Want. It is usually a mindset or belief presented by the protagonist's Normal World (even in most Negative-Change Arcs). The character will likely take this manifestation of the Lie for granted without questioning it much, if at all.

1st Act—The Story's "Small" Introductory Truth: Although the protagonist will spend most of the First Act in a comparative state of tranquility in which the Truth does not proactively contradict the Lie, the Truth will still be present via a "small" introductory version of the story's larger thematic premise. This will often be the thinnest edge of the spear, the first tiny prick of Truth that begins to slowly wedge open a Change-Arc character's awareness of the Lie (which in a Negative-Change Arc will prompt still greater resistance to the Truth).

2nd Act—An Aspect of the Truth Acting as an Antidote to the Specific Lie (Moment of Truth): After the setup of the First Act, the Second Act will represent the protagonist's full-on immersion into the conflict—and, as an extension, his full-on immersion in his inner conflict between Lie and Truth. Throughout the First Half of the Second Act, events will conspire to grant him a growing (if often unconscious) awareness of the Truth.

This finally manifests in the external conflict at the Midpoint, when the character experiences a Moment of Truth. How the character reacts to this revelation will depend on what type of arc he is following. Regardless, the Truth he finds here will not be the complete Big Truth. Rather, it will be a "halfway" Truth of sorts. In order for this thematic revelation to flow properly with the external plot development, the Moment of Truth should be framed as an "antidote" to the specific Lie the character believed in the First Act.

Throughout the subsequent Second Half of the Second Act, the character will not fully reject the entire Lie (or embrace the entire Truth), but he now believes a Lie and Truth that are modified versions of those with which he started out in the First Act.

3rd Act—Remaining "Biggest" Chunk of the Lie: The Third Act can be a tricky time for character arcs. The character needs to have completed most of his growth by this point, but the biggest revelations should remain in order for the Third Act to feel properly climactic. This is why it's important to retain the "biggest" chunk of the Lie for the character to confront in the Third Act. By this point, the character will have embraced *most* of the Truth. But there's still a big mote in his eye. There's still a crucial bit of Lie that he (or, in a Flat Arc, the world around him) hasn't seen past. This will be the Lie's final "argument" within the story.

3rd Act—Climactic Truth: Combating the Third Act's "big chunk of Lie" will be the climactic version of your story's Truth. In essence, this will be the Big Truth of your thematic premise. But it's helpful to refine that Big Truth into the very *specific* Truth needed to resolve your story's main conflict. You can see various ways in which your character will interact with this final Truth, depending on what type of arc he is demonstrating.

How to Find the Right Answers for Any Character's Arc

You almost certainly will not fill in the blanks on this Truth Chart right at the beginning of your story-creation process. Discovering the proper Truth, Lie, theme, and character arc(s) for your story will be an organic process. You won't know the right answers until you first (and simultaneously) have accumulated enough knowledge about your story's plot and your characters' journeys within that plot.

To work well, your story's thematic Truths must emerge organically from every other mechanical piece within the overall structure. Once you're far enough along to know the general shape of your story, you can start looking for its emergent Truths.

Consider what questions your story is asking. For example, some thematic questions I recognized in my own story (which focused on a general theme of *destiny*) while using these tools were:

- Why am I here?

- Who am I supposed to be?

- What is my destiny in this life?

- What is my responsibility in this life?

- What is Life's narrative?

Talk to yourself on the page. What themes do you see emerging? What themes do you want to explore in this story? Try to summarize the theme as a single Truth. You may find several Truths. Keep going, keep refining. Always check yourself against the Truth that emerges in the Climax. How does that Truth tie in within the characters' struggles and misconceptions earlier in the story?

Eventually, you should come up with the single best option for summing up your story's Truth. Hang on to all the other Truths you may have written down because some of them may turn out to be the "smaller" Truths your character will work through in the First and Second Acts, on her way to overcoming the Big Lie and accepting the Big Truth in the Climax.

Truth Chart Examples

To help you see what the Truth Chart looks like in action, here are examples from my own outlining process.

I'm including two different versions of the chart. The first is for the protagonist and therefore represents the story's main theme. The second is for a prominent supporting character. You'll see how her chart riffs off the main Lie/Truth but explores ancillary angles.

Story's Big Truth (Main Theme): What you do matters (and you know what to do).

Story's Big Lie: Destiny is a lie; your life has no narrative, no meaning.

Protagonist/Main Theme Truth Chart

Character's Specific Truth: Responsibility to my truth is my greatest destiny.

Character's Specific Lie: I am not destined to save the world; my actions are all random and some are mistakes.

The Thing the Character Wants: To save the world—and live happily ever after with his love interest.

The Thing the Character Needs: To live a meaningful life.

The Character's Backstory Ghost: The apocalyptic consequences of his mistakes.

1st Act—Specific Manifestation of the "Big Lie": There is no guarantee my actions will turn out for the good.

1st Act—The Story's "Small" Introductory Truth: I can't give up; I have to act.

2nd Act—An Aspect of the Truth Acting as an Antidote to the Specific Lie (Moment of Truth): What I do matters because only I have the abilities to do what must be done.

3rd Act—Remaining "Biggest" Chunk of the Lie: Either Destiny is a set narrative, or life is meaningless.

3rd Act—Climactic Truth: Destiny is inscrutable but still accessible if I am willing, no matter the cost, to listen to my inner truth.

166 | K.M. WEILAND

Supporting Character/Subplot Truth Chart

Character's Specific Truth: My destiny is bigger than my understanding of a narrative.

Character's Specific Lie: The narrative is true, so it must be just me messing it up.

The Thing the Character Wants: To fulfill her narrated destiny.

The Thing the Character Needs: To surrender into the faith and freedom of a larger, more complex acceptance of reality and her place in it.

The Character's Backstory Ghost: Realizing the narrative she had always believed in regarding her destiny was not accurate.

1st Act—Specific Manifestation of the "Big Lie": My destiny is found in my identity.

1st Act—The Story's "Small" Introductory Truth: I must stop denying the truth about reality and my place in it.

2nd Act—An Aspect of the Truth Acting as an Antidote to the Specific Lie (Moment of Truth): If I want to fulfill my destiny, I must give up my stubborn grip on my own identity and my own limited narrative.

3rd Act—Remaining "Biggest" Chunk of the Lie: To fulfill my destiny, I must understand it.

3rd Act—Climactic Truth: The only thing I can do that matters is act in faith.

INTERTWINING PLOT, CHARACTER, AND THEME IN EVERY CHAPTER

In order for plot, character, and theme to create the foundation of story itself, they must be present in every scene.

High-performing stories use scene structure to balance action and reaction on even the micro level in proper scene structure.

In order to execute theme successfully, scene by scene, we have to dive down and take a closer look not so much at scene structure itself, but at how plot, theme, and character interact on the ground level, scene by scene.

Plot on the Scene Level

Plot is the external conflict that moves the story's physical events. At its most basic, plot is what *happens* in the story. The good guy fights the bad guy, gets the girl, hurrah, hurrah. That's plot.

Cohesive plot is executed through application of story structure. There are many different perspectives and explanations of story structure, but all come down to essentially the same thing: pursuit of a goal that arcs through the basic steps of Set-Up, Conflict, and Resolution.

This is the big picture of plot. But what about the little picture? What about plot on the scene level?

Plot is perhaps the easiest part of our story trifecta to double check on the scene level. Because scenes are essentially mini stories of their own, they follow their own structural and emotional arcs. When properly constructed, they form the links that in turn construct the chain of the larger plot.

The best and simplest way to approach scene structure is to view every scene as requiring two halves to make a whole. You can think of these mates as any or all of the following:

- Action>Reaction

- Question>Answer

- Action>Lesson

- Emotion>Opposite Emotion

Although not omnipresent, my favorite remains Dwight V. Swain's classic approach:

Part 1: Scene (Action)

a. Goal (character wants something on the scene level that will ultimately help her reach her overall plot goal—and she tries to get it).

b. Conflict (character is met with an obstacle to obtaining her goal).

c. Outcome (character achieves an outcome to her goal, which is usually disastrous, in the sense that the character does not achieve the intended goal or achieves only part of it).

Part 2: Sequel (Reaction)

a. Reaction (character reacts to the outcome).

b. Dilemma (character must figure out how to overcome the new complications and still move forward toward her main plot goal).

c. Decision (character decides upon a new scene goal to cope with the new complications and move forward toward the main plot goal in a—hopefully—more effective way).

This approach is tremendously useful for the simple reason that it provides both consistent cause and effect and a continuous chain of scenes that all connect one to the other. The Decision at the end of one scene always leads seamlessly into the Goal in the next scene—ad infinitum.

So if your scene structure is perfect, does that automatically mean you're also perfectly executing the plot on the scene level? Yes, it's a good rule of thumb. But no, it's not a guarantee. The guarantee comes into play when you can also verify the following:

- Every scene's Goal is pertinent to the overall plot goal. (This is true even for subplot scenes.)

- Every scene's Outcome moves the plot by changing the plot.

2. Character on the Scene Level

When we speak about "character" as part of the plot-character-theme trifecta of cohesive and resonant storytelling, we're talking about many things.

We're talking about presenting interesting and engaging characters who hold readers' attention. We're talking about developing characters into complexity that resonates within the plot and comments upon the theme. But most of all, we're talking about character as the representative of the shadow side of the plot's external conflict. We're talking about internal conflict.

Once you've chosen an arc for your characters that integrates seamlessly with the plot, how do you make sure you're executing it properly in every single scene?

This is a less logical and less straightforward process than it was to simply apply scene structure to support the plot scene by scene. However, the answer is still inherent in the scene's structure. Specifically, it is found in the *emotional arc* of a scene.

For plot and character to work together, the external and internal conflicts must impact and drive one another. What happens in the external plot must change the character, and what happens in the character's internal conflict must impact the external plot. This mutual impact must happen in every scene.

Just as with plot, the only way to make sure a scene meaningfully incorporates character is to check whether that scene has changed the story.

Examine a recent scene. How has it changed your character?

The change will usually be subtle. If the change is too dramatic, the rapid evolution will either strain suspension of disbelief or end the overall conflict too quickly. Complete change—either internally or externally—signals the end of the story.

Above, we talked about how you can view scene structure in terms of "Action>Lesson" and "Emotion>Opposite

Emotion." Both of these are also keys to nailing down your character's progression in any given scene.

Action>Lesson

It's true that Action>Lesson can apply merely to the story's external process: the character takes an action to implement the scene goal, runs afoul of conflict, and learns something new about how to enact the next goal with more success. However, this is also a useful metric for gauging the character's internal development on the scene level.

Ask yourself:

- How have the events of this scene changed your character's internal conflict?

- What new information has the external conflict provided that gives the character insight into the thematic Truth and/or makes her uncomfortable with the Lie?

- In order for the character's actions to be more successful in the external conflict's next scene, what internal adjustments must be made?

If the answer to any of these questions is vague, you've probably found a scene that hasn't optimally integrated character development and/or advanced the character's arc.

Emotion>Opposite Emotion

Occasionally, it will be appropriate to dramatize an obvious "lesson" for your character, as per the above approach. However, most of the time these "lessons" need to be subtle even to the point of being subtext in order to avoid becoming on the nose and feeling moralistic.

So how do you change your character without being too obvious about it?

As you chart the *external* actions of a scene, make sure your character is *internally* arcing. Never end a scene on the same emotional note as that on which it began. Use the events of the scene to change the character in an obvious emotional way. If she starts the scene happy, end sad. If she starts curious, end satisfied. If she starts depressed, end elated.

Needless to say, the emotions at either end of a scene's spectrum must be organic to the story and must progress the plot. The character can't start out depressed for no reason or end up happy in a way that doesn't force external changes. Her depression at the beginning of Scene 2 must be the result of what happened in Scene 1, just as her happiness at the end of Scene 2 must set up consequences in Scene 3.

3. Theme on the Scene Level

Theme is actually the easiest of the trifecta to implement on the scene level. If you've already successfully intertwined plot and character to the point where they're crucially affecting each other in every scene, then you can be almost positive your theme is also present as the glue holding them together.

Theme on the scene level is rarely as obvious as plot and character. Unlike plot which *is* the scene and character which provides the necessary engine that *moves* the scene, theme is often present only by implication.

If your theme is *love conquers all*, then the concept of *love*, its many variations, and/or opposites will probably be mentioned in only a handful of scenes—or perhaps not at all. But *love conquers all* should still be the unifying idea guiding you in choosing each scene's pertinent action via the character's inner change.

In other words, even if the character doesn't realize it, what he's seeking in every scene is the theme. The ways in which each scene's plot changes the character are direct advances toward or retreats from the story's thematic Truth. If they are not, then you have to question whether that scene's action and character development is actually contributing to the story's overall cohesion and resonance.

The easiest way to double check this is to take a look at the "lesson" and "emotion" in the character section. Do they both relate to the theme?

For example, if the theme is *love*, the character's "lesson" might be as ancillary as "I can't achieve this specific goal without aid from others," while the "emotion" might be gratitude toward a friend who agrees to help or loneliness in the realization that he currently has no loyal friends.

Another actionable way to integrate theme onto the scene level is to look at ways to turn the character's inner battle between Lie/Truth into an externalized moral or philosophical argument. For example, when one of the obstacles in the external conflict is a secondary character's resistance to the protagonist's belief in the way and the why of accomplishing the goal, then the plot itself becomes inherently thematic.

If you've already set up your story trifecta of plot, character, and theme on the macro level of your story, implementing it on the scene level becomes much easier. Optimally, this implementation will grow to be instinctive, taking effect scene by scene as you pull together the pieces of the story into a seamless whole.

"Why are we reading if not in hope
of beauty laid bare, life heightened,
and its deepest mystery probed?"
—Annie Dillard

10

CREATING STORIES
THAT MATTER

THINK BACK TO the books you read and the movies you watched in the last year. Which do you still remember vividly? Which are already foggy?

Now: which type of story do you want to write?

It's a silly question, of course. You want to write stories readers will remember.

There are two types of stories. Stories that are about something, and stories that are *about* something.

As we've seen by this point, plot is an external, visual metaphor for what your story is really about—the story under the story—and theme is the most obvious manifestation of this "understory." Even story subtext that is never brought to the fore, but which still powerfully influences your readers' experiences of the obvious plot, can take your story from "good" to "deeply memorable."

Consider some contrasting examples. We want to look, first, at what these stories are about, and then what they're *about*.

What Is Your Story About on Its Surface?

Stand by Me (directed by Rob Reiner and based on Stephen King's short story "The Body"): On its surface, this beloved coming-of-age story is about a group of four adolescents striking out on a grand adventure in hopes of discovering the body of a missing boy and getting their pictures in the paper.

The Legend of Tarzan (directed by David Yates): On its surface, this film adaptation of Edgar Rice Burroughs's classic character is about an English lord, orphaned and raised in the jungle, who is forced to return to his previous way of life in Africa in order to confront old enemies and protect those he loves.

What's Your Story Really About?

Stand by Me: As with many of Stephen King's stories, the delightful nostalgia and sometimes over-the-top violence and grossness isn't actually the point. The point is the characters' deeper inner journeys, in this case particularly the protagonist Gordie's exploration of life, death, friendship, and growing up.

The Legend of Tarzan: What this blockbuster is about on the surface is *all* it's about. Really, you could stick just about any recent blockbuster in here and find the same regrettable lack of substance. I'm picking on this particular film simply because it had the opportunity to be about more, thanks to the protagonist's unique circumstances and (unrealized) inner conflict. It's telling that within a couple months of seeing it, I could remember hardly anything about it—in contrast to *Stand by Me.*

Your story's "understory" is created from deep and meaningful subtext. You find this by examining your story's plot and asking yourself what greater life questions these external events might logically evoke from your characters.

Ask yourself:

1. If you had to live through the events of your story, what questions of the soul do you think you'd be asking?

2. Then step back even farther and look at your story's big picture. Is the overall conflict a metaphor for something deeper—such as growing up or coming to grips with death?

3. Once you've identified the deeper questions and metaphors offered by your external plot, what can you do to make sure you're making the most of them?

Don't leave your story's best possibilities languishing out of sight. Bring them forward. Use them to strengthen the foundation of your story, to reveal your theme, and to get readers to identify with your characters' struggles.

THE FIVE SECRETS OF GREAT STORIES (THAT WRITERS FORGET ALL THE TIME)

By "great stories," I mean stories that are put together with intelligence, understanding, passion, and vision, giving viewers and readers the opportunity to react to characters and plots that both emotionally engage and intellectually stimulate.

Too few stories offer that level of experience. Part of the reason for this is a corporate mindset (particularly in Hollywood) that hedges its bets with spectacle, instead of risking chips on meaty storytelling. This in turn creates a vicious cycle in which new authors and filmmakers feel this is "the way to do it" and instinctively mimic these patterns. Much of the problem is simply a lack of understanding on the part of those telling the stories.

That's the bad news.

The good news is that, as writers ourselves, we have the opportunity (and the responsibility) to learn from these highly visible mistakes and use them to create better stories. You can start with these five important principles of good storytelling. By "principles," I mean basic storytelling truths that ring true in every story. If you want to write a good book or screenplay, these principles aren't optional. There are more than just these five, of course, but these are arguably the most basic and therefore the most important. They are also the five principles neglected most often in well-meaning fiction that wants to hit the mark but lacks a necessary grounding in strong story theory and application.

1. Every Piece Must Contribute to the Plot

Story is a unit, which requires its various pieces to achieve cohesion. This is true most obviously on the level of plot and structure. Every piece—every scene—must link together, like a circle of dominoes, to create a unified chain of cause and effect. Any extraneous scene or plot twist will, at the least, create a speed bump in your readers' journey through your story.

This is true of more than just scenes and structure. It applies to *every* element in your plot. You should always be looking for ways to repeat motifs, to pay off even the slightest bit of foreshadowing, and to reuse settings and props in thematically meaningful ways. Although most stories can support a *few* loose ends, a good motto for any writer is: *everything matters.*

Characters are the drivers of your plot, but more than that, they are the symbolic and archetypal representation of your theme (something Joseph Campbell famously helped George Lucas implement in the original *Star Wars* trilogy). This means every character must *matter.*

You can't just dream up a cool character, stick him in the story for a few scenes, then write him out or kill him off for no reason. That kind of character is like the nice guy who helps you jumpstart your car and then walks out of your life forever; his contribution to your story makes no lasting impression and his role could just as easily have been played by any other of a million passing strangers.

Structure gives you an easy way to determine whether you've added an integral story element or an extraneous one. The defining moment in any story's structure is the Climactic Moment, which definitively ends the conflict. Everything builds up to this. If you can delete a character, scene, or plot device and still get to your Climactic Moment in good shape—then you don't need that character, scene, or plot device. However cool it may seem or however much fun it may be to write, it is dead weight in your story.

2. Plot Must Contribute to Theme

Just as your Climactic Moment should be the light at the end of the tunnel that guides your every decision about what plot elements to include, your theme should be the lighthouse that guides the plot itself to a meaningful and resonant destination.

Too often plot comes first in stories, and because the storytellers have no idea how to mine that plot for a pertinent theme, they end up, at best, with a scattered mess that fails to offer any important commentary on either the characters' struggles or the viewers/readers' own lives.

This gets even more complex when you realize the more characters and plot lines you're including, the more important it is to weave all this stuff together to reach one meaningful thematic ending for *all* of it.

What is your story trying to say? Every story is saying something. There's no such thing as "just a story." The real question is whether you will dig down into the hearts of your characters, be brave enough and disciplined enough to figure out what it is you're really trying to say, and then do the often messy and difficult legwork of creating character arcs and plot that serve the theme—rather than the other way around.

In his essay in the wonderful anthology *Light the Dark*, Jonathan Franzen offers a challenge to every writer:

> I'm trying to monitor my own soul as carefully as I can and find ways to express what I find there.

3. Stuff Can't Happen Just to Have Stuff Happen

Storytellers notoriously get sidetracked by shiny baubles.

A few years ago, I had the opportunity to read the transcripts from the story-planning sessions in which Steven Spielberg,

George Lucas, and Lawrence Kasdan met to discuss *Raiders of the Lost Ark*. I get an endless kick over how Lucas and Kasdan are calmly working their way through ideas and plots to arrive at the story basically as we know it—and all the while, Spielberg just keeps on throwing in all these wild and crazy ideas, like a little kid having the best time playing make-believe: "Oh, and then you know what would be really cool? We should have a giant boulder come out and squish this guy!"

It's hilarious mostly because it's so relatable. We're all Spielberg. Not only do we want our stories to be as cool as possible for our readers, we're also just really excited about the cool possibilities for ourselves.

But beware of cool. Cool is seductive and can lead far too easily to stories that are chock full of stuff that doesn't matter (Spielberg offered a lot of ideas that *didn't* make it into the movie). Unless it has meaning, cool really isn't that cool.

This temptation is especially dangerous for speculative writers. Science fiction and fantasy's endless possibilities provide us the opportunity to throw in all kinds of cool stuff just because it's cool. But as another Spielbergian character says in *Jurassic Park*:

> They were so preoccupied with whether or not they could that they didn't stop to think if they should.

Why are you adding that gnarly new character? Why did your characters travel to that exotic new setting? Why have you included that funny little subplot? If your primary answer is *Because... it's cool?*, stop and take a second look.

There's no reason you can't include all the cool stuff, but first you must make it matter to the story. It must be so integral to the plot that if you yanked it, meaning would be lost. Even better, it needs to resonate on a thematic level. It needs to offer more than coolness; it needs to either ask questions or provide answers.

There's nothing readers love more than long, complex books or movies... *when they work*. When all that complexity comes together to create the warp and weft of a magical whole, it's too delicious for words. But there's also nothing audiences hate more than long, messy books or movies that drag them through the authors' self-indulgent refusal to recognize and discard meaningless elements. This is even true of stories in which the *pieces* are great but ultimately detract from what might otherwise have been an even better *whole.*

4. Characters Must Change

Okay, I'm harping a lot on *meaning.* Stories must have meaning. But sometimes that seems like a vague directive. Authors are so deep in their own stories, it's often hard for them to know how to look for objective meaning. After all, the very fact that you are writing this thing means it's already meaningful to you.

The single easiest way to determine whether your story as a whole has meaning, or whether any particular element of your story contributes to that meaning, is to look for the arc of change within your story.

Story events that *matter* create change, either in your protagonist or the world around her. Lots of stuff can happen in a story, but if it doesn't affect important and lasting change, then it's just "sound and fury, signifying nothing."

Compare the beginning and ending of your story.

- What's different?

- Which of your characters' beliefs about the world have changed?

- How has this created change in their external actions?

- How have their external actions created change in the world around them?

- How have they changed physically?

- How has the world around them changed physically?

In answering these questions, look past the surface clutter. Maybe your characters fought an epic battle and a bunch of them died. At first glance, that seems like change. But unless that battle has changed your surviving characters' goals or their proximity to those goals, in fact nothing has changed.

This is often a particular challenge in series, since authors need to find a way to bring the protagonist and antagonist into a climactic encounter in every story—without actually ending the conflict until the final installment. But the conflict must be advanced in each encounter; otherwise that particular installment is meaningless within the series.

5. Realistic Cause and Effect Must Arise From Character Motivation

Particularly in a plot-driven story, it can be easy to get so caught up in the external action that you fail to create meaningful character-driven reasons for those actions. You can't have a solid plot without solid character motivations. It simply doesn't work.

Characters can't be at war just because, hey, wars are dramatic and interesting. Characters can't recklessly dive into conflict just because, hey, reckless heroes are awesome. Characters can't fall in love just because, hey, they're both adorable, so why wouldn't they fall in love? The more intelligent and experienced your characters are supposed to be, the more important this becomes.

If your Climactic Moment is the guiding light at the end of the story, then your characters' motivations are the catalyst that sends them in search of that light. Those motivations need to be checked and double-checked in every scene you write. Are your characters making these decisions and executing these actions in total alignment with their mission statements—their motivations—or are they deciding and acting like this just because it's convenient for the plot and will let you stick in some cool "stuff"?

It is the author's foremost (and arguably only) job to serve the story. That starts and ends with crafting meaningful character motivations and then adhering to them with honesty and conviction at every step.

Good storytelling *should* be hard—not because it's impossible, but because it is a high-level skill that requires understanding, insight, energetically clear thinking, and absolute discipline when it comes to choosing elements that will support a worthwhile vision while rejecting those that detract.

As a writer of fiction, you have the ability to use these insights to rise above mediocrity, step into an understanding of the larger world of storytelling, and write weighty stories.

How to Write "Weighty" Fiction

Most authors want to write something that matters. Even if we're never going to win the Pulitzer or be canonized alongside Dickens and Dostoevsky, we still want to know the stories we're spinning are more than just stories. We want them to touch people's lives, make them think, make them question, make them believe. The chief ingredient in any story with that capability is always going to be truth in the form of verisimilitude and a strong thematic premise.

But there's more.

You can create a story steeped in truth and framed upon an excellent premise, and yet it can still fail to feel weighty. When a thematically rich story comes up short in the "weight" department, it just has a feel of... flabbiness. It feels as if it failed to take full advantage of its potential.

Let's examine the five most important factors in creating weight and substance.

Factor #1: Subtext

This is the biggie. No subtext = no depth = no weight.

We talked in Chapter 6 about subtext as the magic ingredient—the sense of the "untold" in a story—the sense of more beneath the surface. Beyond just that sense, the story must offer solid hints and solid questions that can guide readers to using their own imaginations to fill in some of those blanks.

In short, you have to create depth—*and then take advantage of it.*

For Example:

The Right Way to Create Subtext: Ridley Scott's *Gladiator* does a marvelous job with subtext. The weight of the backstory is evident from the very beginning thanks to the skillful and telling interactions between characters who have known each other all their lives. We sense immediately the baggage present in Maximus's relationships with Emperor Marcus Aurelius, Lucilla, and Commodus—as well as between the emperor and his children. That subtext is then paid off throughout the story with just enough deft revelations to explain away our most salient questions without condescending to explain *everything* to us.

The Wrong Way to Create Subtext: Kevin Reynolds's adaptation of *Tristan & Isolde* is a story that brims with potential subtext in the characters' relationships and motivations. Tristan's Ghost (being saved by Lord Marke, who loses his hand in the process and then adopts Tristan) offers potential, but his true feelings about this incident are never satisfactorily developed. As a result, the conflict at the center of the story—between his love for Isolde and his loyalty to Marke—ends up lacking both depth and weight.

Factor #2: Passage of Time

Not that you can't tell a powerful story within a very short timeline, but as a general rule, the longer the timeline in which you have to develop the plot, the more significant the character development will seem. Although it's possible for people to be transformed quickly, most evolutions are the process of time, not least because people require more than one catalyst to prompt change. Consider how much more weight you create by sticking a character in prison for a year versus imprisoning him for only a week or two.

For Example:

The Right Way to Utilize Passage of Time: *Gladiator* covers a significant amount of time as Maximus journeys from the war in Germania to his devastated home in Spain to slavery in Zuccabar to the gladiatorial games in Rome. The passage of time is handled artfully so that it never slows the story's pacing, but rather creates the understanding within us that the character's sufferings are not the fleeting pains of a moment. Thanks to that alone, what he undergoes seems much more important.

The Wrong Way to Utilize Passage of Time: Aside from the ten or so years that pass between the prologue and the main story, the passage of time in *Tristan & Isolde* is never made clear. Tristan's wound seems to heal overnight. The journey from Cornwall to Ireland and back again is performed in a twinkling many times, and we're never given any kind of idea how much time passes after Isolde arrives in England. As a result, the story feels rushed, and the characters' reactions never gain the weight they might otherwise have done.

Factor #3: Multiple Settings

Again, many powerful and meaningful stories take place primarily in a single setting (*The Great Escape* is one of many possible examples). But often you can create a more impressive sense of depth and importance by making sure your plot affects your characters *in more than just one place.*

For Example:

The Right Way to Use Multiple Settings: In self-respecting epic fashion, *Gladiator* manages to traverse almost the entirety of the Roman Empire. Doing so allows us to understand the world in which Maximus lives, the imperial power he faces, and the scope of the population affected by his actions. This works hand in hand with the passage of time to evoke the sense that the character has journeyed far, seen much, and endured many things in pursuit of his goal. Most importantly, the extensive use of settings in this story is never extraneous. The settings are never present simply for the sake of creating epic scope; they serve the plot in a sensible and necessary way.

The Wrong Way to Use Multiple Settings: *Tristan & Isolde* showcases two countries: England and Ireland. But both countries are reduced to two seemingly tiny settings. The lords from all over England frequently gather in Cornwall as if the country were small enough to make their journeys insignificant. The uniting of England is a major theme, but the scope of that problem is reduced significantly in our minds simply because we never get a sense of a *country* rather than a handful of small neighboring villages.

Factor #4: Subplots

Big stories are just that: big. As such, they're about more than just one thing. The character's primary conflict will be supported and contrasted by other concerns—just as our own major problems in real life usually spawn smaller problems. When we reduce a story to a single issue, we eliminate its context and therefore impede its subtext. Thematically pertinent subplots allow us to explore multiple facets of our characters' lives and struggles.

For Example:

The Right Way to Include Subplots: Even though *Gladiator* is an extremely focused story, it still offers many layers. Even though the primary conflict is that of saving Rome, it is Maximus's personal quest for vengeance that fuels most of the plot. The relationships between Maximus and Lucilla, Maximus and Proximo, Maximus and the other gladiators, Lucilla and Commodus, even Commodus and his nephew Lucius—all work together to weave a tapestry of rich contrast and color that would otherwise have been lost if the story were reduced to nothing more than seeking vengeance.

The Wrong Way to Include Subplots: *Tristan & Isolde* offers the opportunity for exceedingly juicy subplots via the relationships of Tristan with pretty much every character in the story. But none are taken advantage of. All the focus is on his relationship with Isolde. Particularly, his crucial relationship with Lord Marke is sadly undeveloped. Even just a single conversation between characters, exploring their motivations in relation to one another, can transform a story.

Factor #5: Emotional and Intellectual Sequel Scenes

Every scene in your story is made of two halves: scene (action) and sequel (reaction). The action in the scene is what moves the plot. But the reaction in the sequel is where the character development and the thematic depth will almost always be found. Never neglect your sequels. For every important event in your story, take time to demonstrate your character's reactions, both intellectually and emotionally. If readers don't know how characters feel about events, they won't be able to properly draw their own conclusions about what to think.

For Example:

The Right Way to Create Sequel Scenes: *Gladiator* didn't win awards because it was an action story. It won critical acclaim because it perfectly balanced its action with strong sequel scenes showing the characters' reactions and emotional processes. When Maximus is visited in his cell by Lucilla after the Midpoint scene when he revealed his identity to Commodus, he reacts by showing his anger, his frustration, his determination, and his sense of betrayal even in regard to her. Without this scene and others like it, his emotional process could only be guessed at.

The Wrong Way to Create Sequel Scenes: The sequel scenes in *Tristan & Isolde* are almost uniformly disappointing. With few exceptions, the characters—especially Tristan—never discuss the intricacies and complexities of their reactions. This is a story that centers around Tristan's conflicted loyalty to a man to whom he owes everything. But that is never touched upon in a satisfactorily direct way. Excellent subtext can only exist when the text itself offers enough meat for readers to chew on.

If you can implement just these five factors in your story—whatever your theme or subject—you'll be able to start crafting cohesion and resonance into your plot and theme.

USING THEME TO CREATE COHESION AND RESONANCE

Because so many pieces must come together to create skillful fiction, it's almost disingenuous to suggest there are only one or two that make or break the story. But if we had to pick just two factors, I think they'd be *cohesion and resonance.*

It's so easy to focus on the big guns—structure, character, theme—that we forget why any of it matters in the first place. The two things that truly matter in fiction—the two things that make or break whether an otherwise well-written story not just works, but kicks everything up to the next level—are cohesion and resonance.

What Is Cohesion?

Cohesion is logic. Cohesion is organization. Cohesion is cutting away the nonessential to find the essential. Cohesion is what happens when everything in a story is there for a reason. Every single part of the story is part of a united whole. It all pulls together seamlessly toward the same end goal.

Cohesion is what you get from a writer who has a specific vision for the story and who works with diligence and discipline to discover the story elements best optimized to support that vision and then pare away all the darlings that distract from it.

Recently, someone asked me to name some of my favorite movies. I started rattling off titles: *The Great Escape, Gladiator, Master and Commander, True Grit, Warrior, Black Hawk Down, Singin' in the Rain, Secondhand Lions, The Bourne Identity, It's a Wonderful Life.* I immediately realized the one commonality in all these stories is a focused and cohesive plot. In fact, the cohesion is so well done in these stories that you almost take it for granted. I certainly do. I don't say, "Oh, I love *The Great Escape* because it's so cohesive." When I'm watching it, studying it, trying to figure out what makes it so powerful for me, I'm thinking more about technical stuff like plot and pacing, character and theme.

But here's the thing: plot, pacing, character, and theme are founded on cohesion. You can have a story that does all those things—even does them well—but if it doesn't bring them together in a cohesive way, the story as a whole will falter and fail.

Granted, it's preferable to have pieces that are better than the whole, rather than pieces and whole that are both problematic. But how much better to write a story that is brilliant because its brilliant pieces came together into a single brilliant whole?

If cohesion is about all the pieces in your story coming together into a unified whole, then the single best place to start that coming-together is with your plot structure. If your story lacks cohesive structure, it will also lack the foundation upon which to execute the rest of your vision.

And, yes, we're back to the idea of vision. To create a cohesive structure, you must know what you want this story to be as a whole. The story must be more than a random collection of dramatic events timed to coincide with the structural beats.

Here are several reminders for when you plot your story:

1. Structure Is the Backbone of Your Story

If you don't have a structure, you don't have a story. What you'll have is just a bunch of stuff happening—and that's if you're lucky. Far too many stories that offer *lots of stuff happening* create next to no actual progression in the plot. Structure is what keeps you on track and assures you're creating a *story* rather than just action.

2. Structural Events Tell You What This Story Is About

Anybody with a little education can structure a plot. But you know you've found a *masterfully* structured story when you can identify all the major structural moments within the narrative (as I do in the Story Structure Database on my site) and see the common elements from plot point to plot point. Nothing is random. It all connects. For example, even though Martin Scorsese's *The Aviator* is a sprawling and varied story, it never loses sight of its structural underpinning via the throughline of Howard Hughes's obsession with aviation.

3. Structural Events Need to Form a Continuous Line of Catalytic Change

The only way to know you're moving the plot is if that plot is *changing*. If events don't force characters to act and react and act again—always changing the story's landscape—then the plot isn't moving and the structure isn't working.

4. The Three Most Important Moments for Keeping Your Structure on Track Are the Inciting Event, the Midpoint, and the Climactic Moment

This isn't, of course, to undermine the importance of other structural moments, obviously. But if you want to verify your structural cohesion (all its parts telling the same story), the first place to look is your Inciting Event (halfway through the First Act), your Midpoint (halfway through the Second Act), and the Climactic Moment (end of the Third Act).

The Inciting Event and Climactic Moment, in particular, should bookend each other; the Inciting Event asks a question which the Climactic Moment directly answers. The Midpoint is the Moment of Truth in between, which redirects the story from the character's understanding of the question in the first half (in both the plot and the theme) to the character's understanding of the answer in the second half.

When it comes right down to it, good structure is all about good foreshadowing—that is, plants and pay-offs. The end is in the beginning. If it is not, then the story isn't cohesive.

What Is Resonance?

A story with cohesion is already far better than most. But cohesion is only half the magic. The other half is resonance.

Resonance is meaning. Resonance is what one of my readers, Eric Copenhagen, called "mythic value." Resonance is what raises a story from interesting anecdote to universal affirmation.

Think about the feeling you get when you connect with a story. That's resonance. That's what we're all looking for, as both readers and writers. Resonance is what lifts a story beyond mere entertainment into an experience of life itself.

Stories without resonance may be fun, but they're quickly forgotten. This is true in any genre. Whether it's a "big" epic journey or a "little" comedy sketch, it won't matter to readers unless it is a mirror reflecting a truth back at them.

Cohesion and resonance go hand in hand because they build one off the other. It's hard to get resonance out of a story that lacks cohesion. Cohesion is the ship in which resonance sails; if it's leaky, the deeper meaning will be at least a little waterlogged. And vice versa: if there's no resonance helming your perfectly cohesive ship, it aimlessly wanders the seas.

Resonance is a little slippery, mostly because it's also a little subjective. Although there are certainly universal truths we all resonate with, there are also specific stories or scenes that affect the individual in ways they do not affect the group. Still, it's pretty easy to spot the stories that didn't get it done in the resonance department: they're soulless.

These are the stories you can just tell had little to no passion behind them. They're stories that were churned out either to make money or just to fit a technically perfect structure (probably both). They're stories that lack imagination, originality, empathy, and courage.

That said, it's entirely possible to be imaginative, original, empathetic, and courageous—and still produce a story that lacks resonance, simply because it wasn't executed well. Like cohesion, resonance only manifests when everything in the story comes together to support a singular vision.

As with cohesion and structure, there is an obvious entry point to checking and refining your story's resonance. By this point in the book, you can probably guess: the entry point to resonance is theme.

It's true that sometimes great themes can arise from poorly structured stories. Usually, this is the result of an author's deep personal awareness and exceptional narrative skill. The bad news is that few writers start out fully equipped with either. The good news is that creating resonance via theme is something you can *learn* to do consciously and deliberately.

If cohesion is intellectual resonance, then resonance is emotional cohesion. Resonance is what you get when you're able to purposefully shape plot and theme to create a unified feeling in your readers. Along the way, you're likely to offer them some interesting ideas to chew on, but even before their brains begin to process all that, they're going to have a sense, a feeling, that, *This works. This is right. This is true.*

If cohesion kickstarts with vision, then resonance kickstarts with honesty. You've created a smart and cohesive plot; now you write your guts out finding its honest core.

Here are a few final pointers to keep in mind:

1. Remember, Theme Is What Your Story Is *Really* About
Resonant stories use their plots to tell the story of the theme, rather than using the theme to simply embellish the plot. Think of plot as the extroversion of the theme. The plot provides the dramatic background that forces characters to physically work through questions of universal truth. The theme and plot are

integrally connected; one always comments on the other. The plot is in many ways a metaphor for the theme, and the theme is likewise a commentary on the plot.

2. Theme Is the Central Existential Question/Answer That Powers Your Plot

Try the trick we talked about in Chapter 2 of boiling your theme down to a central question (e.g., *What is the cost of war? How do we overcome our pasts? Is idealism dangerous?*). A complex story will never be as simple as just one question, but that central question should be your guiding light in choosing cohesive plot elements.

3. Theme Unites Plot and Character

Writers often talk about "plot-driven fiction" versus "character-driven fiction." But truly resonant fiction is rarely either/or. This is because theme is the bridge between plot and character. Character arc explores theme's inner workings, while the characters' actions explore the theme's external realities.

4. Theme Is Not Dogmatic

It is impossible to write a truly resonant story if you believe you have all the answers. This is where the difficult part of being honest comes into play. When you select your story's central question, you must be willing to chase down *all* the possible answers. This doesn't mean you have to believe them all. But it does mean you have to empathize with them enough to play devil's advocate. You must examine all aspects of your question with painful honesty.

Good fiction doesn't insist upon answers; it just asks questions.

Most stories will offer some kind of solution via the protagonist's final choices. But if those final choices are to ring true and give readers something worth thinking about, the journey to the end must be one of empathy.

Cohesive and resonant fiction is thematic fiction. In the midst of all your structuring, character building, and prose polishing, take a moment to check these two all-important ingredients of great fiction off your list. If you can create a story with cohesion and resonance, I guarantee you will have written something truly magical. You will have written something truly thematic.

"There are only two or three human stories,
but they go on repeating themselves
as fiercely as if they never happened."
—Willa Cather

Appendix

THE FIVE MAIN CHARACTER ARCS

YOU CAN FIND many different approaches to story theory that break down the number of "human stories" into different categories. One of the most powerful approaches—one that unites plot and theme—focuses on character arc.

A basic way to look at character arcs is to learn about the two Truth-driven or heroic arcs—the Positive-Change Arc and the Flat Arc—and the three Lie-driven or Negative-Change Arcs—the Disillusionment Arc, the Fall Arc, and the Corruption Arc.

As I mentioned in Chapter 2, I've talked about all these arcs extensively, beat by beat, in my book *Creating Character Arcs* and its accompanying workbook. As a refresher for those already familiar with character-arc theory and a primer for those who are new to it, this appendix offers a basic structural beat sheet for each arc.

THE SIX FOUNDATIONAL INGREDIENTS OF ALL CHARACTER ARCS

All five arcs share commonalities, beginning with their foundational structure (broken into three acts and ten beats, as you'll see once we start analyzing the actual arcs). Beyond that, they also share the six foundational ingredients, which can then be tweaked to the author's needs according to whichever arc has been chosen for the story. These foundational ingredients are:

1. The Thematic Truth

Your story's Truth is your thematic principle. It is a universal statement about how the world works. In almost all instances (with the arguable exception of the Disillusionment Arc), the Truth will represent an ultimately positive (if sometimes painful) value, which will help the characters interact more fruitfully and less futilely within the world.

2. The Lie the Character Believes

The Lie is a misconception about the world that contrasts the Truth. At the beginning of the story, the Lie will be preventing someone (either the protagonist or, in the case of the Flat Arc, supporting characters) from seeing, understanding, and/or accepting a necessary Truth. The entire character arc—and indeed the entire story—is about if and how the character(s) will be able to evolve past the Lie into the Truth.

3. & 4. The Thing the Character Wants vs. the Thing the Character Needs

The inner thematic conflict of Truth versus Lie will manifest in the external plot conflict as the Thing the Character Wants versus the Thing the Character Needs. Usually, the Need is nothing more or less than the Truth, although it can take a physical form as well. The Want may be something large and abstract (such as "respect"), but it should boil down to a very specific plot goal (e.g., "a promotion" or "a college degree"). Your character's evolving proximity to the Want and the Need will change in direct relation to the specific character arc.

5. The Ghost

The Ghost (sometimes referred to as the Wound) is the motivating catalyst in your protagonist's backstory. This is the reason the character believes in the Lie and can't see past it to the Truth. As its name (coined by John Truby) suggests, the Ghost is something that haunts the character, something that can't just be moved past. Often, it is a traumatic event, but even something seemingly positive (such as a parent's pride in a child) can cause a character to believe a limiting Lie.

6. The Normal World

The Normal World is the initial setting in the story's First Act, meant to illustrate the character's life before the story's main conflict. Depending on the type of arc, the Normal World will symbolically represent either the story's Truth or the story's Lie. The Normal World may be a definitive setting, which will change at the beginning of the Second Act when the character enters the Adventure World of the main conflict. However, it may also be more metaphoric, in which case the setting itself will not switch, but rather the conflict will change the setting *around* the protagonist (e.g., changing the atmosphere from friendly to hostile).

THE TWO HEROIC ARCS

The Positive-Change Arc and the Flat Arc are the "happy" or "heroic" arcs. In these stories, the protagonist either learns or already knows the Truth—and uses it to positively impact the story world.

1. The Positive Change Arc

Character Believes Lie > Overcomes Lie > New Truth Is Liberating

The First Act (1%-25%)
1%: The Hook: Believes Lie
The protagonist believes a Lie that has so far proven necessary or functional in the existing Normal World.

12%: The Inciting Event: First Hint Lie Will No Longer Work

The Call to Adventure, when the protagonist first encounters the main conflict, also brings the first subtle hint that the Lie will no longer serve the protagonist as effectively as it has in the past.

25%: The First Plot Point: Lie No Longer Effective

The protagonist is faced with a consequential choice, in which the "old ways" of the Lie-ridden First Act show themselves ineffective in the face of the main conflict's new stakes. Although the protagonist does not yet recognize the inefficacy of the Lie, he will still pass through a Door of No Return, in which he is forced to leave the Normal World of the First Act and enter the Adventure World of the main conflict in the Second Act.

The Second Act (25%-75%)
37%: The First Pinch Point: Punished for Using Lie

The protagonist is "punished" for using the Lie. In the Normal World, he believed he could use the Lie to get the Thing He Wants. But in the Second Act, this is no longer a functional mindset. Throughout the First Half of the Second Act, he will try to use his old Lie-based mindsets to reach his goals and will be "punished" by failures until he begins to learn how the world really works.

50%: The Midpoint (Second Plot Point): Sees Truth, But Doesn't Yet Reject Lie

The protagonist encounters a Moment of Truth in which he comes face to face with the thematic Truth (often via a simultaneous plot-based revelation about the external conflict). This is the first time the protagonist consciously recognizes the Truth and its power. He does not yet, however, recognize the Truth and the Lie as incompatible. He will attempt to use both in the Second Half of the Second Act.

62%: The Second Pinch Point: Rewarded for Effectively Using Truth

The protagonist is "rewarded" for using the Truth. Building upon what he learned at the Midpoint, the protagonist will start implementing Truth-based actions in combating the antagonistic force and reaching toward the Thing He Wants. He will be "rewarded" by successes as he moves nearer and nearer his ultimate plot goal.

The Third Act (75%-100%)

75%: The Third Plot Point: Rejects Lie

The protagonist is confronted by a "low moment" brought about by his continuing refusal to fully reject the Lie. Finally, the protagonist must confront the true stakes of what he stands to lose if he continues to embrace the Lie. Feeling all but defeated, he rejects the Lie. Implicitly, he also fully embraces the Truth.

88%: The Climax: Embraces Truth

The protagonist enters the final confrontation with the antagonistic force to discover whether or not he will gain the Thing He Wants. Directly before or during this section, he consciously and explicitly embraces and wields the Truth.

98%: The Climactic Moment: Uses Truth to Gain Need

The protagonist uses the Truth and all it has taught him about himself and the conflict to gain the Thing He Needs. Depending upon the nature of his Truth, he may also gain the Thing He Wants, or he may realize he must sacrifice it for his own greater good. As a result, he definitively ends the conflict between himself and the antagonistic force.

100%: The Resolution: Enters New Truth-Empowered Normal World

The protagonist either enters a new Normal World or returns to the original Normal World, where he can now live as a Truth-empowered individual.

2. The Flat Arc

Character Believes Truth > Maintains Truth > Uses Truth to Overcome World's Lie

The First Act (1%-25%)

1%: The Hook: Believes Truth in a Lie-Ridden World

The protagonist believes a Truth that the rest of the Normal World around her rejects. The Normal World and most of its characters are mired in a central Lie which enslaves them in some way.

12%: The Inciting Event: Challenged to Use Truth to Oppose Lie

The Call to Adventure, when the protagonist first encounters the main conflict, presents a direct challenge to her Truth. The question at this point is whether or not she can be convinced to take action in wielding her Truth against the Lie of the world around her.

25%: The First Plot Point: World Tries to Forcibly Impose Lie

The protagonist is faced with a consequential choice, in which the antagonistic force attempts to forcibly impose the Lie upon her or others. In refusing to relinquish her Truth for the Lie, the protagonist passes through a Door of No Return, in which she is forced to leave the Normal World of the First Act and enter the Adventure World of the main conflict in the Second Act.

The Second Act (25%-75%)

37%: The First Pinch Point: Uncertain if Truth Is Capable of Defeating Lie

The protagonist struggles to use her Truth against the strength of the antagonistic force's Lie. She experiences doubt about whether her Truth is capable of defeating the Lie and, as a result, if it is indeed the Truth.

50%: The Midpoint (Second Plot Point): Proves Power of Truth to World

The protagonist perseveres in following her Truth. She offers a Moment of Truth to the world around her. This is the first time the protagonist will demonstrably exhibit the full power and purity of the Truth. At least one significant supporting character will be impacted (positively or negatively) by this revelation.

62%: The Second Pinch Point: Lie-Driven Characters Fight Back

In response to the protagonist's powerful demonstration of Truth at the Midpoint, other Lie-driven characters will double down on the Lie and use it to mount a formidable counter-attack upon the protagonist and her Truth.

The Third Act (75%-100%)
75%: The Third Plot Point: Lie Seems to Triumph Externally

The Lie-driven tactics of the antagonistic force hit the protagonist hard, even to the point of the protagonist's seeming defeat in the external conflict. The protagonist is confronted by a "low moment" brought about by the supporting characters' continuing refusal to fully reject the Lie. The protagonist must confront the true stakes of what she stands to sacrifice if she continues to embrace the Truth. Even in the face of overwhelming odds, she reaffirms her conviction of the Truth.

88%: The Climax: Final Confrontation Between Truth and Lie

The protagonist enters the final confrontation with the antagonistic force to decide whether or not she will gain the Thing She Wants. She consciously and explicitly embraces and wields the Truth.

98%: The Climactic Moment: Truth Defeats Lie
The protagonist uses the Truth (often with the help of positively changed supporting characters) to defeat the antagonistic force and gain the Thing She Wants and Needs (which are often the same thing in a Flat Arc, since the protagonist always possesses an understanding of the Truth).

100%: The Resolution: New Truth-Empowered Normal World
The protagonist enters a new Normal World, which is empowered by the Truth thanks to her actions.

THE THREE NEGATIVE CHANGE ARCS

Stories are about change. Sometimes that change is positive, driven by hopeful or even heroic people. But sometimes that change is negative, driven by humanity's darkest urges and blindnesses, as we see in the three Negative Arcs—the Disillusionment Arc, the Fall Arc, and the Corruption Arc.

1. The Disillusionment Arc

Character Believes Lie > Overcomes Lie > New Truth Is Tragic

The First Act (1%-25%)
1%: The Hook: Believes Lie in Comfortable Normal World
The protagonist believes a Lie that has so far proven necessary or functional in the existing Normal World, which is often a comfortable and complacent place.

12%: The Inciting Event: First Hint Lie Is Untrue
The Call to Adventure, when the protagonist first encounters the main conflict, also brings the first subtle hint that the Lie will no longer serve the protagonist as effectively as it has in the past.

25%: The First Plot Point: Full Immersion in Adventure World's Stark Truth

The protagonist is faced with a consequential choice, in which the comfortable "old ways" of the Lie-ridden First Act show themselves ineffective in the face of the main conflict's new stakes. The protagonist will pass through a Door of No Return, in which he is forced to enter the Adventure World of the main conflict in the Second Act, where he is confronted by a stark and painful new Truth.

The Second Act (25%-75%)

37%: The First Pinch Point: Punished for Using Lie

The protagonist is "punished" for using the Lie. In the Normal World, he was able to use the Lie to get the Thing He Wants. But in the Adventure World, this is no longer a functional mindset. Throughout the First Half of the First Act, he will try to use his old Lie-based mindsets to reach his goals and will be "punished" by failures until he begins to learn how things really work.

50%: The Midpoint (Second Plot Point): Forced to Face Truth, But Unwilling to Embrace It

The protagonist encounters a Moment of Truth in which he comes face to face with the thematic Truth (often via a simultaneous plot-based revelation about the external conflict). This is the first time the protagonist consciously recognizes the Truth and its power. He is, however, horrified by the implications of this dark new Truth. Although he can no longer deny the Truth, he is unwilling to fully embrace it or to surrender his comparatively wonderful old Lie.

62%: The Second Pinch Point: Growing Frustration With Old Lie and Disillusionment With New Truth

The protagonist is forced to confront consistently increasing examples of the Lie's lack of functionality in the real world. He grows more and more frustrated with the Lie's limitations. He begins to accept the horrible Truth. He is profoundly disillusioned by his new worldview, even as he begins to be "rewarded" for using the Truth to reach for the Thing He Wants.

The Third Act (75%-100%)

75%: The Third Plot Point: Accepts That Comforting Lie Is Now Completely Nonexistent

The protagonist is confronted by an irrefutable "low moment," in which he can no longer fool himself that the dark Truth is not true. He must not only accept this new Truth, he must also admit that his comforting old Lie is now completely nonexistent.

88%: The Climax: Wields Dark New Truth in Final Confrontation

The protagonist enters the final confrontation with the antagonistic force to decide whether or not he will gain the Thing He Wants. Directly before or during this section, he consciously and explicitly embraces and wields the dark new Truth.

98%: The Climactic Moment: Fully Acknowledges Truth

The protagonist uses the Truth and all it has taught him about himself and the conflict to gain the Thing He Needs. Depending on the nature of his Truth, he may also gain the Thing He Wants (only to discover that, in light of his new knowledge, it is worthless), or he may realize he needs to sacrifice it for his own greater good. As a result, he definitively ends the conflict between himself and the antagonistic force.

100%: The Resolution: Disillusioned With New Truth

The protagonist either enters a new Normal World or returns to the original Normal World, but with a jaded eye now that he knows the Truth.

2. The Fall Arc

Character Believes Lie > Clings to Lie > Rejects New Truth > Believes Worse Lie

The First Act (1%-25%)

1%: The Hook: Believes Lie

The protagonist believes a Lie that has so far proven necessary or functional in the existing (often destructive) Normal World.

12%: The Inciting Event: First Hint Lie Will Not Save or Reward

The Call to Adventure, when the protagonist first encounters the main conflict, also brings the first subtle hint that the Lie will no longer effectively protect or reward the protagonist in her current circumstances.

25%: The First Plot Point: Lie Now Completely Ineffective; Makes Move Toward Truth

The protagonist is faced with a consequential choice in which the "old ways" of the Lie-ridden First Act show themselves ineffective in the face of the main conflict's new stakes. The protagonist is given an early choice between old Lie and new Truth. She passes through a Door of No Return, in which she makes a move toward the Truth and, in so doing, is forced to leave the Normal World of the First Act and enter the Adventure World of the main conflict in the Second Act.

The Second Act (25%-75%)

37%: The First Pinch Point: Halfhearted Attempts at Truth Only Half-Effective

The protagonist tries to wield the Truth as a means of gaining the Thing She Wants, but does so only with limited understanding or enthusiasm. She is stuck in a limbo-land where the old Lie is no longer a functional mindset, but where her halfhearted attempts at the Truth prove likewise only half-effective.

50%: The Midpoint (Second Plot Point): Glimpses Truth, Rejects Truth, Chooses Worse Lie

The protagonist encounters a Moment of Truth in which she comes face to face with the thematic Truth (often via a simultaneous plot-based revelation about the external conflict). This is the first time the protagonist consciously sees the full power and opportunity of the Truth. However, she also sees the full sacrifice demanded if she is to follow the Truth. Unwilling to make that sacrifice, she rejects the Truth and chooses instead to embrace a Lie that is worse than the original.

62%: The Second Pinch Point: Lie Is Effective, But Destructive

Uncaring about the consequences, the protagonist wields her Lie well and finds it effective in moving toward the Thing She Wants. However, the closer she gets to her plot goal, the more destructive the Lie becomes both to her and to the world around her.

The Third Act (75%-100%)

75%: The Third Plot Point: Complete Failure to Gain Either Want or Need

The protagonist is confronted by a "low moment," in which she experiences a complete failure to gain the Thing She Wants. This failure is a direct result of the collective damage wrought by her Lie in the Second Half of the Second Act. The "means" caught up to her before she reached her "end." However, even when faced by all the evidence of the Lie's destructive power, the protagonist still refuses to repent or to turn to the Truth.

88%: The Climax: Last-Ditch Attempt to Salvage Want

Upon entering the final confrontation with the antagonistic force, the protagonist doubles down on her Lie in a last-ditch attempt to salvage the Thing She Wants.

98%: The Climactic Moment: Total Destruction

Crippled by the Lie (in both the internal and external conflicts), the protagonist is unable to gain the Thing She Wants (or gains it only to discover it is useless to her). Instead, she succumbs to total personal destruction.

100%: The Resolution: Aftermath
The protagonist must confront the aftermath of her choices. She may finally and futilely accept the inescapable Truth. Or she may be left to cope, blindly, with the consequences of her choices.

3. The Corruption Arc

Character Sees Truth > Rejects Truth > Embraces Lie

The First Act (1%-25%)
1%: The Hook: Understands Truth
The protagonist lives in a Normal World that allows for or even encourages the thematic Truth. As a result, the protagonist starts out with an understanding of the Truth.

12%: The Inciting Event: First Temptation of Lie
The Call to Adventure, when the protagonist first encounters the main conflict, also brings the first subtle temptation that the Lie might be able to serve the protagonist better than the Truth.

25%: The First Plot Point: Enters Beguiling Adventure World of Lie
The protagonist is faced with a consequential choice, in which he is enticed out of the First Act's safe, Truth-based Normal World into the Second Act's beguiling, Lie-based Adventure World. Not realizing the danger (or believing he is weighing the consequences), the protagonist is lured through the Door of No Return by the promise of the Thing He Wants.

The Second Act (25%-75%)
37%: The First Pinch Point: Torn Between Truth and Lie
The protagonist is torn between his old Truth and the new Lie. The Lie proves itself effective in moving him nearer the Thing He Wants. But he wages an internal conflict as he recognizes he is moving further and further away from his old convictions and understandings of the world.

50%: The Midpoint (Second Plot Point): Embraces Lie Without Fully Rejecting Truth

The protagonist encounters a Moment of Truth in which he comes face to face with the Lie in all its power. He recognizes he cannot gain the Thing He Wants without the Lie. Although he is not yet willing to fully and consciously reject the Truth, he makes the decision to fully embrace the Lie.

62%: The Second Pinch Point: Resists Sacrifice Demanded by Truth

The protagonist is "rewarded" for using the Lie. Building upon what he learned at the Midpoint, the protagonist will start implementing Lie-based actions in combating the antagonistic force and reaching toward the Thing He Wants. The Truth pulls on him, demanding sacrifices he is not willing to give. He begins resisting the Truth more and more adamantly.

The Third Act (75%-100%)
75%: The Third Plot Point: Fully Embraces Lie

The protagonist utterly rejects the Truth and embraces the Lie. He acts upon this in a way that creates a "low moment" for the world around him (and for him morally, even if he refuses to recognize it). He is now willing to knowingly endure the consequences of rejecting the Truth in exchange for what he sees as the rewards of embracing the Lie.

88%: The Climax: Final Push to Gain Want

The protagonist enters the final confrontation with the antagonistic force to decide whether or not he will gain the Thing He Wants. Unhampered by the Truth, he pushes forward ruthlessly toward his plot goal.

98%: The Climactic Moment: Moral Failure

The protagonist uses the Lie and all it has taught him in an attempt to gain the Thing He Wants. He may gain the Thing He Wants and remain senseless to the evil engendered by his actions. Or he may gain the Thing He Wants only to be devastated when he realizes it wasn't worth what he sacrificed. Or he may fail to gain the Thing He Wants and be devastated by the realization that his sacrifices to the Lie were fruitless. One way or another, he definitively ends the conflict between himself and the antagonistic force.

100%: The Resolution: Aftermath
The protagonist must confront the aftermath of his choices. He may turn away from the Lie, admitting his mistake and accepting the consequences. Or he may callously forge ahead, intent on continuing to use the Lie to further his own ends.

***

Needless to say, there are many variations of these arcs. But if you can identify and master these five, you're well on your way to writing a powerful evolution that will resonate with readers.

Note From K.M. Weiland: Thanks so much for reading! I hope you've enjoyed learning how to create powerfully thematic stories. Did you know that reviews are what sell books? If *Writing Your Story's Theme* was helpful to you, would you consider rating and reviewing it? Thank you and happy writing!

Want more writing tips?

CLAIM YOUR FREE BOOK!

REFERENCES

Bird, Matt, "Parallel Characters in *Sunset Boulevard*," <http://www.secretsofstory.com/2013/11/rulebook-casefile-clones-in-sunset.html>

Gardner, John, *The Art of Fiction* (Random House, Inc., 1983)

Franzen, Jonathan, *Light the Dark*, edited by Joe Fassler (Penguin Books, 2017)

Hauge, Michael, *Writing Screenplays That Sell* (Collins Reference, 2011)

Mussel, Eric, *A Writer's Space* (Adams Media, 2008)

Margulies, David, *The Writer*, October 2015.

McKee, Robert, *Story* (HarperCollins, 2010)

Phillips, Melanie Anne; Huntley, Chris, *Dramatica* (Write Brothers Press, 1999)

Truby, John, *The Anatomy of Story* (Faber and Faber, Inc., 2007)

Truby, John, "Truby Rates the Oscar Hopefuls – 2016," <http://truby.com/truby-rates-the-oscar-hopefuls/>

ABOUT THE AUTHOR

K.M. WEILAND LIVES in make-believe worlds, talks to imaginary friends, and survives primarily on chocolate truffles and espresso. She is the award-winning and internationally published author of the popular writing guides *Creating Character Arcs*, *Outlining Your Novel*, and *Structuring Your Novel*, as well as the gaslamp fantasy *Wayfarer*, the dieselpunk adventure *Storming*, and the portal fantasy *Dreamlander*. When she's not making things up, she's busy mentoring other authors through her award-winning blog Helping Writers Become Authors. Visit her on Facebook or Twitter to participate in her Writing Question of the Day (#WQOTD). You can email her at kmweiland@kmweiland.com.

Also by K.M. Weiland

Is Structure the Hidden Foundation of All Successful Stories?

Why do some stories work and others don't? The answer is structure. In this award-winning guide, you will discover the universal underpinnings that guarantee powerful plot and character arcs.

Powerful Character Arcs Create Powerful Stories

Look deeper into the story beats that create realistic and compelling character arcs. Learn how to achieve memorable and moving character arcs in every book you write.

Think being a superhero is hard?
Try being the first one.

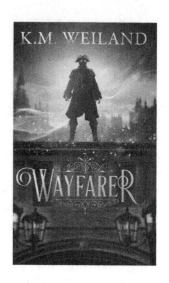

Sometimes even pilots
have to wing it.

What if dreams came true?

KMWeiland.com

Acknowledgments

My profound thanks to the patrons of Helping Writers Become Authors!

Kim Ashby

Natalie Barelli

Rebecca J. Bastian

Tyson Beck

Cindy Bergquist

Denise Yoko Berndt

E.G. Bertran

Taryn Blackthorne

Bobby3

Susan Bogan

Evelyn Breithaupt

Christy Burdick

David Butler-Groome

Terry Carlson

Charsierism

Jackie Casey

Andy Clark

Terrence Cleary

Gordon Conochie

Joel Davison

Arabella Dawn

Kristen DeClemente

Laredo Dixon

Sharon Duncan

N.R. Eccles-Smith

Bob Fox

Susan Geiger

Debora Habsburg

Christopher Halk

Natasha Hanova

Happy Hatterson

Frances K. Hill

Parker Hudson

Chalon Hutson

McNeil Atticus Inksmudge

Joking611

Richard Jones

Ramona G. Kearney

Renee Leonard Kennedy

Nin Leavitt

Kelly Larivee

Usvaldo de Leon

Lise

Marie

William Marden   Maureen Wood

Robert J. Mendenhall

Susana Morais

Jack Mulcahy

Joseph Nastanski

Frank Nichols

Erik Nord

Jenny North

Travis O.

Sabrina M. Paltz

Katrina Pavlovich

James Rehg

Jada Rowland

Emmeli Runesson

Soleah Kenna Sadge

Saskia

Louis Schlesinger

Sevali

Leslie K. Simmons

Jason Stonecipher

Graham Spiers

Victor Thong

Eric Troyer

Melina Wedin

Marnie Werner

Derek Wheeless

Also by K.M. Weiland:

A Man Called Outlaw

Behold the Dawn

Dreamlander

Storming

Wayfarer

Non-Fiction

Outlining Your Novel

Outlining Your Novel Workbook

Structuring Your Novel

Structuring Your Novel Workbook

Creating Character Arcs

Creating Character Arcs Workbook

Jane Eyre: The Writer's Digest Annotated Classic

Conquering Writer's Block and Summoning Inspiration

5 Secrets of Story Structure

Made in the USA
Monee, IL
30 March 2021